The Bronx Trilogy

Three books of poetry inspired by The Bronx

the shoe shine parlor poems et al
concrete pastures of the beautiful bronx
from the banks of brook avenue

W R Rodriguez

zeugpress

The three books of *The Bronx Trilogy* are presented here in one collection.

The original type size and pagination for each of the books has been retained.

The second edition of *the shoe shine parlor poems et al* was selected: it includes a bibliography of previous publications and a preface that discusses the book and introduces the trilogy.

The colophon that appeared as the final page of *from the banks of brook avenue* has been replaced with an acknowledgments page: "Bibliography: Previous Publications."

The Bronx Trilogy by W R Rodriguez

Print Editions
the shoe shine parlor poems et al. Ghost Pony Press, 1984.
the shoe shine parlor poems et al: second edition. Zeugpress, 2016.
concrete pastures of the beautiful bronx. Zeugpress, 2008.
from the banks of brook avenue. Zeugpress, 2016.

Electronic Editions
the shoe shine parlor poems et al. Zeugpress: Smashwords Edition, 2014.
the shoe shine parlor poems et al: second edition. Zeugpress: Smashwords, 2016.
concrete pastures of the beautiful bronx. Zeugpress: Smashwords Edition, 2014.
from the banks of brook avenue. Zeugpress: Smashwords Edition, 2015.

© 1984, 2008, 2014, 2015, 2016, 2019 w r rodriguez

All rights reserved

Printed in the United States of America

ISBN: 978-0-9632201-6-5

zeugpress

the shoe shine parlor

poems et al

w r rodriguez

zeugpress

Grateful appreciation to the Mary Roberts Rinehart Foundation for supporting the completion of the original manuscript.

And thanks to Robert Stern for his friendship over the years.

The first edition of *the shoe shine parlor poems et al* was published by Ghost Pony Press in 1984.

> **Acknowledgments:**
>
> Poems from this book appeared in the following magazines and anthologies:
>
> *Abraxas, Bronx Accent: A Literary and Pictorial History of the Bronx; Collage of 9 & 1; The Croton Review; Editor's Choice III: Fiction, Poetry & Art from the U.S. Small Press (1984-1990); Epoch; Fistflowers: Poems of Struggle and Revolution; I didn't know there were Latinos in Wisconsin I; I didn't know there were Latinos in Wisconsin II;* and *The U.S. Latino Review.*

Second Edition

© 1984, 2016 w r rodriguez
All rights reserved

Printed in the United States of America

ISBN 978-0-9632201-4-1 *(the shoe shine parlor poems et al second edition)*

zeugpress

Contents

Preface to the Second Edition of *the shoe shine parlor poems et al* vii

I
the shoe shine parlor poems

making it	11
the cop	12
the shoe shine poem	13
al's pictures of old times	14
grandfather	16
coffee	17
blinky	18
the banana man	20
little spic & big man	21
the bust	24
jim	25
the long walk to bed	26
private rivers	27

II
et al

the moon does not linger	31
Something Fishy	32
the miracle	34
the old woman	35
late one hot august	36
the day i threw thoreau off the roof	37
they disappear	38
of bootblacks	40
what i remember most about hughes avenue	41
the accordion player	42
butch	44
weeds	46
the bronx at the end of the mind	47

Bibliography: Previous Publications 48

dedicated to my parents and to my wife

"The cover photograph, taken in about 1929, shows my aunt, my grandfather, three uncles (two biological, one adopted) and several customers."
— w r rodriguez

Preface to the Second Edition of *the shoe shine parlor poems et al*

This book is dedicated to my parents and to my wife, and rightly so. My mother liked to talk, and passed on family stories, in elaborate detail, to me and to a variety of cousins. My father, whose family suffered through the Great Depression, and who worked his way up from office clerk to office manager, did nothing to stop me from avoiding a career in banking, or from foregoing engineering and declaring myself an English major. My wife does not define happiness and fulfillment in terms of money. If she did, she probably would not have married someone who wanted to write poetry.

Without assimilating my mother's sense of detail, I do not know if I could write the way I do. Without my father's tolerance of my youthful decisions, I might never have become a teacher of high school English, which allowed me to pay the bills while pursuing my interests in literature and writing. And my wife, going to poetry readings and reading revisions of my work, has been my best emotional support and editorial guide over many years.

I wrote the first poem, "making it," in a Bronx laundromat. I was in college and living at home. Watching the family laundry spin around seems an appropriate context for the poem's inspiration. When I moved to Wisconsin, I began writing "the cop," "blinky," "the bust," and "jim." Like much of my work, they are based on true stories, but I often change the names of the leading characters. I was influenced by the Beats and by the Romantics, and it occurred to me that The Bronx was a worthy subject for poetry.

Among the first in my family to attend college, I had moved from the tenements of The Bronx to attend graduate school at the University of Wisconsin-Madison. Having started my career as a bootblack, I was somehow fulfilling the Great American Dream. It seemed fitting to call my first book *the shoe shine parlor poems et al*.

The cover photograph, taken in about 1929, shows my aunt, my grandfather, three uncles (two biological, one adopted) and several customers. After the riots of the 1960s, the glass windows were replaced with plexiglass portholes bolted into plywood. By the 1970s, sneakers, sandals, and vinyl shoes made their impact, and the shoe shine parlor's income declined.

My uncle recruited me into the family business when I was eleven. I began by washing the shoes. After several months I was entrusted with completing the entire shine. Shining shoes is often looked down on in America. But it is an honest job. One works hard, sees the results of his labor, and is paid and given a tip. I was proud of being a bootblack. I built muscle, learned to interact with people, and used my savings to pay my share of college tuition. And I got to learn what was going on in the neighborhood without being directly involved.

So being a bootblack, and listening to my mother, and having a tolerant father, and an understanding wife (who also grew up in the South Bronx and who also was an English major) enabled me to write this book. I am indebted to these blessings, and also to Ingrid Swanberg, whose Ghost Pony Press published the first edition of *the shoe shine parlor poems et al* in 1984.

Much has happened in the decades since the first appearance of this book. My parents have passed. My children have grown and moved on. The Bronx has been rebuilt. I retired from teaching, but three decades of producing a high school literary magazine taught me how to do layout and gave me some practice in editing. In 2008, I spent the summer learning how to use a new layout program. I did this by producing the sequel to *the shoe shine parlor poems*. I entitled it *the concrete pastures of the beautiful bronx,* and published it under my Zeugpress imprint. I decided then that I wanted to complete a trilogy of books about The Bronx and the urban experience. The third book, *from the banks of brook avenue,* is being released in 2016. My wife has been very gracious in reading and commenting on numerous revisions of the poems.

As the trilogy is completed, I am reprinting a limited number of copies of *the shoe shine parlor poems et al.* Though my work has evolved over the decades, I remain pleased with this book, and the text is the same as that of the first edition. I simply want to have enough copies to complement *the concrete pastures of the beautiful bronx* and *from the banks of brook avenue* when I offer *the bronx trilogy* to my readers.

I remain most grateful to Ingrid and to Ghost Pony Press and to all those who have supported and influenced my work over the years.

w r rodriguez
January, 2016

I

the shoe shine parlor poems

making it

great grandfather burned some government office
in some spanish town   made it to puerto rico
hiding in jungles   huts   from wanted posters
& police   must've hid pretty well because

somehow grandfather made it to new york
rolling cigars   surviving the depression   & me
putting dirt in his pipe   sitting always
by the television   watching yankee games
never cheering   smiling sometimes
dying in a railway flat
on cypress avenue where he lived twenty years
in the south bronx

where my mother also lived   forty years
met my father   married   sent him to wall street
each day dressed in the suit he wore
even on saturdays

while she stayed home
remembering to me her father   the handsome
little italian   who also made it to philadelphia
then to new york   the south bronx   sweeping speakeasies
founding the family business

                              the shoe shine parlor
i worked there seven years   sweating
reading plato's symposium   tristram shandy
playboy magazines between shines
not speaking spanish or italian but laughing anyway
at the customers' dirty jokes

                              never listening
even if they spoke english   mind never there
body pushing brushes   burning two-&-a-half-cent cigars
mind someplace else   in riverdale   la rive gauche
in bed with the playmate of the month
in that spanish town a hundred years ago
but always

someplace else

the cop

one week he was a movie star
dyed his hair blond   quite unusual
for a puerto rican   & he strolled
up & down 138th street   smiled
gave autographs   & occasionally
a 3×5 glossy

suddenly he was a cop   the only one
i ever saw walk a beat in our neighborhood
138th & 137th   brook avenue   saint ann's
even brown place   in a regulation blue uniform
shoes shined   night stick twirling   a tin badge
& cap guns in a cowboy holster

every night he guarded the newsstand till it closed
got a free paper   & walked the newsman home
saturday afternoons the children followed him
the men who sat on milk boxes   playing dominoes
drinking beer   talking about the cock fights
would yell   *hey officer*   & ask directions
to places they were not going
or tell him of cars double parked around the corner

but he was a nice cop   gave accurate directions
did not give tickets
& when the streetlights went out   he directed traffic

when the riots came   in the summer of 67
or 68   probably both   he was there
in the middle of 138th street   with a riot helmet
& his dime store guns   with five or six
hundred other cops   who chased the crowds up the block
or were chased   or who stood in doorways
watching the stores   dodging bricks   while he sat
on a friend's car so it would not be overturned

once in a while someone would shout
rotten pig   & throw bottles at him
but they were always aimed to land
ten or twenty feet away
& i never saw a cop   smile
so much in a riot

the shoe shine poem

i tell ya man
i finished the shine
& as he got off the stand
i saw a gun in his belt

i started praying
as he reached for his wallet

then he gave me
a buck
& told me to keep the change
& i said to myself

my prayers are answered

i ain't had a buck shine in a month

al's pictures of old times

a boxer doing an l sullivan pose
three men in two piece bathing suits drinking beer
our shoe shine parlor back in the '20s
when there were stands outside too
& uncle giaco was there
& grandpa
funny calling him grandpa
because i never met him

& i don't remember giaco
except ma would tell me
how skippy howled every midnight
for six months after the car
killed him

he wasn't really our uncle though
my grandparents took him in
when he was just off the boat
& he became a relative
worked in the parlor with al
opened up every morning at six
washed down the marble stand
& polished the brass footrests
six or seven days a week

went back to italy once
a month after his mother's funeral
but mussolini wanted to draft him
he had been a runner for general pershing
& that was war enough for him
so he stayed on the ship
came back to brook avenue
& years later was run over by a car
crossing 138th street to buy us ice cream

& snapshots of faces i didn't know
but al remembered
*one or two of them gangsters
in the '30s they would sit on the stand*

& polish their guns
al said
while he shined their shoes

photos of cats & dogs & cousins
a drill sergeant & some cops
aunts & uncles
old christmasses & customers
all turning yellow
behind the dusty glass

grandfather

his father was an exporter
so it wasn't as hard for him to leave italy
as it was for a lot of others   & work
his way up the coast   florida to phillie
bought land there with his brothers-in-law
had a barber shop   & a store   on main street too
but he left it   all in a family argument
returned only for funerals   & weddings
the old fashioned kind   with buffets   home pressed wine
virgin brides

he made it to new york   with his wife
& the children they had on the boat   & in various other states
then in manhattan my   mother   the ninth & last
not counting the two who died of pneumonia & tb
all living in a cold water flat by the polo grounds
then in the south bronx   right around the corner
from the shoe shine parlor he bought
in the early '20s

               worked it with his sons
swept streets   & speakeasies on the side
bartended after the repeal   had as much fun
as anyone during the depression   went fishing & crabbing
in pelham bay before it was polluted   & sometimes
on sundays   treated ma to a ride on the third avenue el
& once a year   took the whole family for a picnic
sailing the dayliner to bear mountain

               but mostly he worked
ten or twelve hours a day   came home   took a short nap
woke   went for a walk   returned with the paper
read it & made sure his daughters were home by nine

he never let his children curse   & never
let anyone call him a son of a bitch
would say   *i've got a real mother*   & fight to prove it
only time he'd ever fight   & he usually won
once he even got hit over the head with a barstool
but he proved he had a real mother anyway

two days later   he collapsed behind the bar
his friends   carried his corpse
home   in a chair

coffee

a small man with a twisted body
five feet three
a size six shoe
& the other a four
so it wasn't much trouble
to give him a free shine
while he spoke to al

not really talk
but al understood his
choked sounds & gestures
& understood almost everybody
no matter what language they spoke
or smiled & pretended to

we helped coffee on & off the stand
when he came around on saturday afternoons
or sunday mornings after church

he usually brought al coffee
sometimes smelled of whiskey

& was always happy

blinky

had a glass eye that didn't fit well
but he was too poor to get another
so folks called him blinky   the one eyed junkie
because he was a junkie   & twitched a lot
trying to keep his eye from falling out

he wasn't like the other junkies who weren't like him
& who hung around   wasted   waiting to score
watching who to rob   & mugging people
angel's father's head bloodied   stabbed in the chest too
not because he fought back   but because they wouldn't take chances
or waste time asking   & in a rush they pushed maria
who lived next door & was seventy-six years old
down the stairs   took her pocketbook   the social security money
just enough to pay the rent   & buy thirty dollars food each month
she spent ten weeks in the hospital   with fractured ribs
& a broken hip   so they could get their fix
but blinky wasn't like them

maybe he didn't have much of a habit to support
or maybe he dealt on the side
but he'd just hang around the supermarket
carry packages home for a quarter or half-a-buck
take odd jobs   paint apartments
sweep sidewalks   bring down the garbage for the super
in bad times he'd beg by the subway

one night blinky overdosed in some basement
folks said he didn't move an eyelid
when the cops carried him to the ambulance

word got around he was dead
someone painted a cross on the sidewalk
put a bouquet of plastic flowers next to a hat
read the bible & took a collection   *for blinky's funeral*
he said   & the old women walking home from the stores
dropped in dimes & quarters
some stopped to listen to the prayers

two weeks later blinky returned
he woke up in lincoln hospital   stole some clothes & walked out
right past the cops & nurses   back to 138th street hoping for a fix

when he saw the cross still painted on the sidewalk
& found out about our donations
he had some fine ideas on spending the money
so he & a few friends went looking for the man who took the collection

but no one could ever find him

the banana man

looked like jimmy durante
had a room on 139th street
worked for d loi & sons
trucking bananas all over new york

got a free shine every saturday
gave us a huge bag of bananas
talked a while about the flats & trots
then took the bus to belmont or the big a

worked all the overtime he could
saved his money
& spent his vacations at saratoga

little spic & big man

little spic
the name he was known by   but a person
could only speak it with affection   little spic
wasn't shorter or taller   or bigger & meaner
or cooler & mellower than anyone else
& he didn't try to be

                                          he just held his own
through tough times   struck hard   ran fast
when he had to   now he was the old timer
of the block   & drove the smoothest bus
in the bronx   *too old to turn from anything*
he joked with the passengers

                              & no taxi
ever beat him in a fair race   he knew enough
of the ways of the world to negotiate
translate or otherwise assist a friend in need
through any crisis from a wedding or a funeral
to football tickets & the recovery of stolen or confiscated property

he had many friends   never sought enemies
earned his title in grammar school during the '20s
when the irish & italian & german kids who ruled the streets back then
would rough him up & get him down   until one day
he grabbed the biggest guy by the collar
shook his head a few times & said   in a fierce voice   *yeah*

i'm little spic   so what of it   that bunch
never troubled him again   they became buddies
& stuck up for each other like brothers
they were as tough as they had to be to survive
& as lucky   they lived according to the code of their pride
never crossed a friend   never struck from behind

or without good reason   they never took nothing
from those who had nothing   & that was more than could be said
for the loan sharks   local politicos   & insurance agents
who sold bogus policies   promises   & quicksand loans
to depression families   *it's a hard life*
people are strange   little spic thought

& no matter how many friends he might make
he knew that some folks would always   if only
in a small but certain way   think of him as just
a little spic   so he figured he'd get the jump on them
any way he could   no friend of his
ever used his christian name again

                          & during the depths
of the '30s his drinking buddies passed him a good tip
about a rough job   & they worked together until the war
driving trucks in the garment district   which is where
they learned the old trick of carrying a lead pipe in a rolled up newspaper
to fight off hijackers

               & thirty years later
when he walked home late that friday night from the bus route
he got in '47   he had a foot long rod of bicycle frame
in an evening news to fend off muggers   & so when big man
who was not so big he didn't have to prove his muscle
& who was known to prefer the pleasure of assault & battery

to the profits of pure thievery   staggered up to little spic
& grabbed his throat yelling   *you damn ricans
i'm gonna kill allaya   & bury you in jersey*   little spic
afraid it might be the last thing he'd ever do
swung his newspaper with all his might   & walked away with no hurry
leaving big man unconscious on the sidewalk

but he didn't get too far when a police car drove up
& one of the cops yelled   *hey old man
what happened to that big guy over there*
& little spic said   with no hesitation
*i don't know   he was walking around real drunk
& he just collapsed*

& the other cop yelled to two young guys
who were sipping a pint in a doorway across the street
hey what happened to that big guy over there
& they answered with no hesitation
he was walking around real drunk   said one
he just collapsed   said the other

well that's as good as any place to sleep it off
muttered the cop at the wheel as they drove away

& little spic walked home to the wife who always waited up for him
& the two guys kept sipping their pint until all was clear
then they crossed the deserted street & walked up
real quiet

      to big man who was snoring drunk on the sidewalk
nose up jowls drooling sprawled beside some trash cans
& boxes & bags of garbage with a touch
light as a fly his wallet was lifted he never woke
so holding their noses they stole his shoes
& biting back laughter threw them beneath a car

big man snored on in his stupor so they slipped off his pants
threw them upon a nearby fire escape & split to spread the news
a hundred folks soon gathered *let's take a good look
at this strong mouthed giant who seems to have insulted one too many of us
for his own health* someone said loudly in spanish & it was a sight
because big man wore no underwear that night

& it wasn't long till the laughter woke him the crowd moved back
big man swayed to his feet & stretched a bit until he realized
he was standing surrounded in the street
so he reached to a pocket for his knife in case there was trouble
& jolted when he felt his bare skin
they're on the fire escape yelled a little kid

big man ran to the fire escape as the crowd opened around him
he ain't so big shrieked a woman from her window
& big man tried leaping to reach his pants he couldn't jump too high
because of his hangover but he kept trying anyway
the crowd became hysterical big man went berserk
& tackled some guy around the waist yelling *give me your pants*

give me your pants *give me your pants* until three cops drove up
& grabbed him but he got one in a bear hug still yelling
give me your pants *give me your pants* as more cops dragged him away

& even after he jumped bail he was never seen in these parts again
though his name was remembered in stories & drunken ballads
which in our neighborhood always ended with the moral

you don't mess around with little spic

the bust

i knew bo & bub   the two detectives who busted frank
they came in for a shine   drunk every friday night
never tipped   & seldom paid us   not like the other cops
not like the pimps & bookies who'd give bills
& say   *keep the change*

once bub told georgey   as he sat next to him on our stand
that they almost caught him stealing that mustang last night
& would get him the next   bust his ass too
but georgey laughed & said they wouldn't

& i sure wish i'd pounded   the brush into a corn or bunion
because frank never did nothing
except box in the golden gloves   train all day
walk his dog at night   & look a little
like georgey the rat king   who was doing lots of things

but it was frank they arrested   tackled him crossing 138th street
cuffed him & drove him down by the river
to the alley beside the furniture warehouse
where they beat him with blackjacks   held guns to his head & said
they'd shoot him & throw him in the harlem river

then they kicked frank & beat him with their pistols
until two patrol cars drove up to arrest them
but bo & bub identified themselves   so they all brought frank
to be booked with grand larceny   petty theft   resisting arrest
& several counts of assault & battery upon officers of the peace

the dog came home alone & frank's mother was worried
but a few neighbors ran in yelling   *frank's just been busted*
so they rushed to the police station
& sat there three hours before frank arrived
& even then the desk sergeant wouldn't let his mother see him
or send for a doctor   until some friends
got a manhattan lawyer to take the case   free of charge

now bo & bub shine their own shoes   they're doing two to five
frank's walking a little dizzy   he can't fight no more
& georgey the rat king   is still   doing lots of things

jim

i was thirteen   there wasn't much to do on those sticky august nights
except listen to the yanks drop two to the twins
look out the window   maybe see a star or two
& catch the latest on the all night outdoor poker game
when suddenly   thirty or forty guys turned the corner
from saint ann's avenue   came right down 138th street
ripping off car aerials   slashing tires
throwing bottles at a stray dog

the gamblers grabbed their beer & abandoned their milk boxes
as the gang hurled trash cans through store windows
set woolworth's on fire   carried off a few televisions
& strolled away laughing into the night

ten minutes later the cops & firemen arrived
people looked from their windows to see what had happened
& our super   old jim   was sweeping the gutter
when a cop walked up   & bashed his head with a night stick

maybe he thought old jim was one of the gang
& couldn't run fast enough to escape
or maybe he thought old jim pulled off the whole riot by himself
but i don't know because no one ever saw that cop again
& jim wasn't arrested   just taken to the hospital
& let out two weeks later with a bandaged head & a broken nose
& went right back to work   sweeping hallways & collecting the garbage

folks would see him & ask   *how you doing jim*
& tell him he should go to the civil liberties union
find out who that cop was   & sue him   sue the city too
but i knew jim wouldn't

              & he didn't
he was an old black gentleman   grew up in virginia
when i was a boy   we couldn't walk on the sidewalk
if white folks was walking on it   had to walk in the gutter
he told me one day while i shined his shoes

& now he just said   *i can't sue that cop*
it wouldn't help my head none
besides   that cop is the law
i was brought up to obey the law
& i'm too old to change

the long walk to bed

my footsteps echo down empty streets. the moon is full, but the stores are hidden behind steel roll down gates, & the shoe shine parlor is boarded over with plywood. the trash cans are in their usual places, & patches of black ice are unmoved by the wind. it does not snow much anymore, but the night is very damp, & cold. in my building, rusted icicles hang from the hallway radiator. they are a month old & still growing. i dream of nothing, shivering in my sleep, cold as a parking meter.

private rivers

private rivers
is dead   he stepped
on a mine   on the wrong road
in a mistaken land   in an old war   his young
dogtagged blood exploded   & dried brown upon green
backed leaves   that rotted in the chemical breeze

private rivers   is dead   he wound up
on the wrong road   the gossip goes
because the illiterate corporal   could not read the map
to the literate lieutenant who could not read maps
& was actually an actuary   & the old sergeant
had retired yesterday   & the new sergeant had not yet been delivered

& the platoon radio was not working
so the lieutenant   who never took advice from noncoms
could not consult the captain who had chronic gout & never left the base
& the major was on leave   & the general
at the peace talks   did not hear the explosion
but signed the letter anyway

the wake was a closed coffin   flag & flowers
affair   fat priests   babies bawling to be fed
nervous brothers   pale sisters   some pfc's
a corporal in a wheelchair   the grandmother
prayed & cried & shrieked her grief
& the widow fainted at the cemetery

private rivers is dead   the news spread
& shattered our neighborhood
he was a seventh son   never known
to be in the wrong place at the wrong time
or to leave a poker game empty handed   never robbed   never arrested
never beaten by a crazy cop   & he was always lucky

playing the numbers   until they drew him
a seven in the draft lottery   & now
everyone was nervous   the patriotic eulogy
no consolation   *how would life deal to us*
spoke up a drunk gambler
if it didn't leave enough of him to fill a coffin

27

II

et al

the moon does not linger

the moon does not linger
in this neighborhood

naked as a silver dollar
she sneaks out from behind a building
or a cloud of smoke

and hurries west
into the suburbs of new jersey
or the corporate farms of quiet kansas

leaving the poor lunatics
madly staggering
or dreaming amid constellations
of streetlights
counting
their fortune

Something Fishy

Be the first on your block!
the ad proclaims
Wear our new Prodigal Princess shoes!
    Clear plastic!
        Happily hyper-elevated!
           With gold buckles
and a real live goldfish in each heel!

Here she comes—
the first to obey the commanding black majuscules.
She smiles
    proud as a successful fisherman.
Like Ahab she limps
    bitten by the sharp gold buckles.

She sails across the street
buoyant on the real live goldfish
    whose reflection she watches
unaware of the red light
    and the speeding white bus
        now spouting its horn.

Full speed ahead
she escapes the thrashing king of rolling highways
    but her left shoe
        broken at the buckle
           does not.

The fish
    though constantly trying
cannot swim through the plastic
    until the heel is crushed.
Then he flies freely through the air
    graceful as a sea gull
        an albatross
           an erne.
He falls to the asphalt
    wiggles his tail in dead earnest
        and dies.

Lamenting the price of the shoes
cursing the bus

she hobbles on the surviving heel
and sinks into the crowd of shoppers.

The fish rests on his side.
One eye
    always open
        stares
            at the sky.

the miracle

jerry knelt outside the church. eric hid behind a pillar on the loggia. as an old woman walked by, jerry yelled: *oh god, please send me a pair of sneakers.* a slightly used pair of sneakers fell into jerry's waiting hands. the old woman's eyes opened wide. she was about to kneel when eric, barefoot, came down the stairs and smiled. the old woman raised her cane. jerry scrambled to his feet and began to run, but the old woman just shook her head and tapped her cane on the sidewalk. and laughed.

the old woman

through the window the world hangs
painted shut long ago
brown
with grease and dust
a lifetime of his smoke
and her cooking with garlic

the great
great grandmother sews
in time to the clock's ticking
stitches which hold
everything together

the empty birdcage shivers in a draft
his pipe cold upon the ashtray

she draws her shawl
embroidered with canaries
and flowers

children playing in the distance
her fingers
are nimble
still

late one hot august

late one august
so hot and sticky it seemed
september would never come
late one hot august
in the fireplug's frigid spray
a girl splashed naked and young

late one hot august
while a clutched beercan cooled the hydrant's roar to a hiss
and rainbows bubbled over cobblestones
late one hot august
a fountain arched silver to the sky
and fell

late one hot august
when numb fingers let the bent can slip
and sprawling the child flung far into the street
late one hot august
a passing coal truck
crushed her head like an eggshell
late one hot august
her unborn life ran out
late one hot august
and rippled with the currents
late one hot august
and sank into the sewers
late one hot august
of brook avenue

the day i threw thoreau off the roof

was three days after a riot, was two days after our mayor toured the property damage, was a day after the radio told me i lived in a slum, was my first day off work in months. the day i threw thoreau off the roof, was a hot day which melted the tar, was another day of the mosquitoes which bred in the backwater of the sewer our city would never fix and bit anything that could still bleed. the day i threw thoreau off the roof, was the angry day i refused to do my homework, was the happy day i watched yellow pages flutter down the airshaft like poisoned pigeons. the day i threw thoreau off the roof, was not up to civil disobedience, was just sick of reading about those damn beans.

they disappear

day and night they disappear
lovers of smiles and moonlight and swollen dolphin bellies
that shoot like stars over the waves
whispering
a birth
a birth

they disappear
some beaten on side streets in the afternoon
while the children are in school studying history
some dragged screaming from their lovers' arms
before the newborn moon can open its eye

they disappear
are hidden underground where there is no green utopia
are left to slow death in the gray world
are chained naked to dank walls and nibbled by desperate rats
are denied the tomb's comforts

they disappear
although some are allowed to return after many years
with beards and volumes which are read and reviewed
sold underground or catalogued in the library of congress
although some organize rape workshops
some fight for the poor
and some whose constitutions permit it preach
in parks to squirrels and pigeons

they disappear
no
grendel the great fen monster has not eaten them
no
singing fairies have not carried them away
no

hands with knives and guns and government papers
are taking them
hands with blackjacks and chains and cattle prodders
are taking them
hands shaped like fists
are taking them

voices of many languages
condemn them
curses in barrooms and on bronx streets
condemn them
military juntas and corporate conspiracies and terrorist kidnappings
condemn them
condemn them
condemn them
and they disappear

soon
there will be no one left

of bootblacks *(for al)*

the eyes of bootblacks
do not see where shoes go
after they walk out of sight

the foreheads of bootblacks
recall the hides' stains
and soles worn beneath the buff

the hair of bootblacks
is every color
their backs droop with the growing strength of age

the arms of bootblacks
snap the rag's rhythm as hours dance
their feet seldom travel
yet are weary with the day's journey

the mouths of bootblacks
tell no lies
and speak the world's tales

the ears of bootblacks
hear all within earshot
even when they do not listen

the hands of bootblacks
are calloused where brush joins flesh

their art is to pound
the grin of a thunderbolt
onto a landscape of bunion
and crease

what i remember most about hughes avenue

where retired italians sweating in beach chairs
watch tides that never come

what i remember most

and midnight's nomads drift through the christmas wind

what i remember

that torrid apartment with walls of ice

what

is moments of twilight with you in my arms
a candle dancing upon a ceiling

there is joy among our shadows

we are lulled
to the flickering

and we
for
get

the accordion player

he is gone   that gray haired man
with the roman nose   who bellowed up airshaft
and alley   down street and avenue
songs the old folks knew   and danced
and seemed young forever in the immortality of music

he is gone   that arm swaying man
who tipped a gray cap   who smiled and skipped
fingered and squeezed the air
as if a virgin   who bed the wind in a box
as a loud deity

he is gone   who panned the gray windows
and ears of this iron city like a god   embarked
from the foothills of a golden time   shedding wordless ditties
that rustle migrant memory to a younger day
an older way   and the children were happy

silver   nickel   copper   pure from the outstretched arms
of the barely poor   too heavy with work
too thin with youth   to pump music from the grind and drone
the clatter and chatter of the trolley shaken cobblestones
and the crescent white belly through the orchard street suit   bulges

earns a mortal living   while crowds gather in groves
on hot streets   squinting   stunned after the gloom
of hallway and bedroom   the fruits of labor
ringing and clinging through the applause
rolling round the thick soled shuffle of his feet

or they stare   obscure paintings behind windowpanes
crooked in their frames   lining the long thoroughfares
and the stagnant airshafts   those interior courtyards
four walls of splotched mortar and rough cut brick
the cracked pavement below   a square of sky above

and the weatherbeaten clotheslines of the crisscrossed world between
drooping diapers and bedsheets that cry   underwear
dripping clean from the sweat of love   or they lean
from the worn sills of endless edifices   brown or maroon   ash or cream
crumbling crockets long rooted in brick   grave with the unique venations
       of life

a husband   a wife   baby in a bib   wrinkled women in grease
     bellied frocks
yank open the venetian blinds   plaid skirted high school girls
fondling lockets and dime store pearls   unshirted men   tattoos
and cigars   crucifixes   garlic cloves   a few scars
and everywhere the eyes of children

watch notes and chords rise   leaves on the updraft of a wild dream
burst from bustling esplanade and shaded yard   past corniced facades
where sparrows nest among the lotus and rosette of the festooned modillion
past spires and crenelations and the common copings of tile and stone
past patched tarpaper rooves and pigeons circling endlessly home

he is gone   that gay eyed man with the baggy clothes whom no spring
will ever return   who shuffled away while the sun swooped low
a breeze blew up the street   and the verdure burned with autumn
he is gone   into the miasmas of music   gone

butch

in darkness before the bronx sunrise when the fighting does end
    when the screaming side streets die down to damp silence
    when shattered glass embeds itself in dull memory

when sticks no longer swing   when the knife's flash
    no longer sparkles the guttural and shrieks of rabid snarling men
    and hysterical women   and illuminates the laughter
    and cries of wide eyed children

in darkness when bullets lie cold in graves of flesh and brick

in darkness when time is too quiet   he sets it right
and his cry echoes down the night
btchooooooooooooooooooooooooooooooooooooooooooooooooooooo
btchooooooooooooooooooooooooooooooooooooooooooooooooooooo

in darkness between the two suns and after fortune takes its daily toll
    after winners and losers shuffle home from curbside poker games
        that spiralled like a chant from sunset   long into the late night

after the midnight stickball champs share their last beer
    after the ivory dominoes are polished with a white cloth
        and entombed in black leather   after the crapshooters' prayers
        and dances roll to a death rattle   and the clicks
        and mutterings bury themselves in catacombs of tenements

in darkness when the gambling is done the clawed cock's feathers
    rise from the corpse in the wind

in darkness when time is too quiet   he sets it right
and his cry echoes down the night
btchooooooooooooooooooooooooooooooooooooooooooooooooooooo
btchooooooooooooooooooooooooooooooooooooooooooooooooooooo

in darkness between time's snake eyes dawns the dim light
    of forgotten childhood's crystalline afternoons
    before the gypsy cab strikes   before fresh blood
    casts like prophecy over iridescent asphalt   and the mind's shell
    cracks upon the squared sidewalks of concrete reality

dawns the din of young afternoons   shouts of red rover
    red-light-green-light-1-2-3   skullcap   skullcap   skullcap
    running the hot streets   before brainsurgeons aping mortality
    drive metal plates like the cadillacs of civilization
    into the sprawling alleys of the run down psyche
    and the unfortunate soul is rescued from heavenly high rises
    which shine amid eternal streetlights
    beyond the wheelings and dealings of the stars

in darkness the urchins' sunny jeers
in darkness the lips refuse to close

in darkness when time is too quiet   he sets it right
and his cry echoes down the night
btchoooooooooooooooooooooooooooooooooooooooooooooooooooooo
btchoooooooooooooooooooooooooooooooooooooooooooooooooooooo

in darkness   in the crevice between two moments
    before the cock crows   before a trace of twilight
    fades the unseen east   after the starry pitch
    stained to the depths the night   and the moans
    of distant lovers strangled in sleep

when i stare into my own restless darkness

a silhouette in an unlit window
    a burning voice
                that certain eye
                             through the night
btchoooooooooooooooooooooooooooooooooooooooooooooooooooooo
btchoooooooooooooooooooooooooooooooooooooooooooooooooooooo

weeds

we are weeds

we are everywhere weeds who stand together and grow in lonely places
    where grass and trees will not

we are ancient weeds who have multiplied and sent our children
    upon the four winds to the polar wastelands and to the jungles
    and deserts of the great solar circle

we are strong weeds sweating at dawn   sick weeds choking on pesticides
    toiling weeds who grasp the rich earth   brittle weeds who wither
    beneath dry suns

we are wise weeds who fear bulldozers

we are sad weeds who watch cities rise like tombstones from the graves
    of our ancestors

we are many weeds who litter the lots of abandoned landlords   who loiter
    upon the renovated window boxes of graffitied brownstones

we are penniless weeds deposited along broken riverbanks where the corporate
    surplus flows to the ocean's vault

we are swaying weeds who crawl around factories   who are contaminated
    at industrial parks   erased in college campuses   and burnt upon
    suburban lawns

we are lofty weeds stranded on rooftop islands of soot   reckless weeds
    whistling between railroad ties as trains pass   carefree weeds
    in the city's eroded parks   dancing

we are restless weeds who creep through the concrete's cracks like banshees
    from the green underworld   who wail the foreclosed land where all share
    the earth's poverty   who moan in the wind   who bask in the sun
    who eat the soil   who drink the rain

we are weeds

we dream of freedom

the bronx at the end of the mind

each day clutching
on steeple and sill
of factory and office

the soot grows black

fire escapes rust
subways roar   rocking foundations
cracks in the pavement
flow wide   fast   free
and empty
into the gnarled tides
which gnash the cement shores
of this god trusting land

the stench that crawls from the sludge
wanders like a swart thought
through this harbor city

night calls the ghosts of spice
fried fish and incense
to dance out the windows

again the feast

our singing drowns the sea

Bibliography: Previous Publications {the shoe shine parlor poems et al}

the accordion player
Editor's Choice III: Fiction, Poetry & Art from the U.S. Small Press (1984-1990). The Spirit That Moves Us Press. 1992.

blinky (selected lines)
Bronx Accent: A Literary and Pictorial History of the Bronx. Rutgers University Press. 2000.

the cop
I didn't know there were Latinos in Wisconsin: An Anthology of Hispanic Poetry. Friends of the Hispanic Community. 1989.
Fistflowers: Poems of Struggle and Revolution. (An anthology for the University of Wisconsin-Whitewater's Spring Poetry Festival.) 1988.
Epoch. Vol. 26, no.3, spring, 1977.

the day i threw thoreau off the roof
I didn't know there were Latinos in Wisconsin: 30 Hispanic Writers Volume II. Focus Communications. 1999.

grandfather (selected lines)
Bronx Accent: A Literary and Pictorial History of the Bronx. Rutgers University Press. 2000.

little spic & big man
I didn't know there were Latinos in Wisconsin: An Anthology of Hispanic Poetry. Friends of the Hispanic Community. 1989.
Fistflowers: Poems of Struggle and Revolution. (An anthology for the University of Wisconsin-Whitewater's Spring Poetry Festival.) 1988.
Abraxas. Vol. 27/28, 1983.

making it
Collage of 9 & 1. The Bronx Council on the Arts Inc. 1973.

the moon does not linger
Croton Review. Vol. 1, no. 3, 1980.

private rivers
I didn't know there were Latinos in Wisconsin: An Anthology of Hispanic Poetry. Friends of the Hispanic Community. 1989.
Fistflowers: Poems of Struggle and Revolution. (An anthology for the University of Wisconsin-Whitewater's Spring Poetry Festival.) 1988.

they disappear
I didn't know there were Latinos in Wisconsin: An Anthology of Hispanic Poetry. Friends of the Hispanic Community. 1989.

weeds
The U.S. Latino Review. Issue 1, winter-spring 2000.

concrete pastures

of the beautiful bronx

w r rodriguez

zeugpress

Poems from this book previously appeared in:

The Critic; Dusty Dog; "I didn't know there were Latinos in Wisconsin" Volume II; North Coast Review; The Party Train: A Collection of North American Prose Poetry; Poets on the line; Turnstile; Two Worlds Walking: Short Stories, Essays, & Poetry by Writers with Mixed Heritages; and *Welcome to Your Life: Writings for the Heart of Young America.*

Selections from "roosevelt's bust," "logic," and "saint mary's park" appeared in: *Bronx Accent: A Literary and Pictorial History of the Borough*, Lloyd Ultan and Barbara Unger (Rutgers University Press: 2000).

Also by w r rodriguez: *the shoe shine parlor poems et al* (Ghost Pony Press: 1984).

© 2008 w r rodriguez
All rights reserved

ISBN: 978-0-9632201-2-7 *(concrete pastures of the beautiful bronx)*

Printed in the United States of America
First Edition

Zeugpress

Contents

I
the bootblack 7
my little red fire engine 8
sledgehammer man 11
the spectacle 12
the cockfight bust 13
logic 14
the great american motorcycle boots 15
democracy 16
they told me not to sing 18
the malthusian theory 21
beyond the window 22

II
nightmare off bruckner boulevard 25
webster avenue 26
scratch park 27
off southern boulevard 28
the dharma express 29
the bronx vikings 30
jonas 31
gouverneur morris laughs from his grave 32
beyond the crying tenements 34

III
roosevelt's bust 37

IV
saint mary's park
    fuzzy caterpillars 49
    lost playgrounds 52
    the seasons before 54
    rosebud 56
    flesh and blood 57
    the trees of saint mary's 58

V
pastoral esplanades 67
ferry point park 68
the subway grating fisherman 70
maples forever 71
crossing invisible streams 72
saint jude's bazaar 76

Bibliography: Previous Publications 80

*to mary ellen, annemarie, and robert,
and to robert and marguerite—
thank you*

I

the bootblack

the bootblack
neither
creates the shoe
nor kills the cow

has no theories
but the preservation
of leather
and the soul's thin hide

burnishes a small
part of the world
pounding wonder
from the mundane

clodhoppers
loafers
wing tips
combat boots

the legendary
puerto rican fence climbers
pumps and
police brogues

reality is unique
as a world worn foot
these walking streets
are beautiful

my little red fire engine

my little red fire engine
i sit i steer i pedal
toward imaginary disasters
as though i were important
but today no kids are out
to save from the flames
too hot this august morning
for many emergencies
this holy day of obligation
at early mass the stone walls
of saint luke's church
chill the bronx heat
señoras in black dresses
finger rosaries
the last irish knights of columbus
guard lonely pews
priestly latin drifts
through the morning peace
firemen beside the holy water
on the threshold are ready
to scramble but the alarm
does not ring
the offertory bells
startle all to salvation
hook and ladder 29
just across the street
its art nouveau facade
wondrous to a young boy
searching for heroes
and glory
engines shiny
freshblood red behind
a trinity of corniced arches
prepared to rescue all
from mortal infernos

nothing burns
devotional candles melt with prayer
the priest's homily
is in the vernacular
heaven is heaven and hell is hell
earth is the mystery to me
o for the paradise years
before riots and assassinations
and the arson that burns
through the safety of sleep
brickbats bottles the rage of the mob
greet the saviors
so many willing to throw stones
at so few
before despair there is hope
which flickers away
save the apartments we desperately need
the building beside the church
is torched one winter night
the top two floors lost
before the ladder is raised
five stories overhead the lone fireman
directs the hose
he is a silver angel
in the white spotlight
the orange flames
the black sky
the brown smoke
it is all just another insurance payout
a cheap eviction of unwanted tenants
this is the incense
of the church of the bronx
charred tenement skeletons
stand like sentinels of death
acres of crumbled brick and broken glass

fill for years with garbage
weeds grow amidst the rot
faint promise of a green life
the trash is set ablaze
these are the prairies of the slums
where wild dogs scavenge
and there is wailing
and gnashing of teeth
we make our offerings
and we eat the divine
we are blessed and are sent
into the stark sunlight
of bronx streets
at the bakery the cinnamon buns
are still warm
mother perks the coffee
and sends me out to play
in my shiny red
little fire engine
and i roar up and down
but the arsonists are sleeping
and there is no one to save

sledgehammer man

i need a couple bucks he says
sleeveless white tee shirt
skinny muscles
that sledgehammer props him up
that sledgehammer says maybe he'll bust up the place
his friend smiling like something nice gonna happen
he's scowling
i need a couple bucks
and i don't know what to say
i just see that sledgehammer
i need a couple bucks
and uncle reaching towards the cash register for his billy club
i need a couple bucks
and cousin whips a lead pipe
from beside the radiator and says
you're not getting any money
you're not getting any money
and they walk away
the smiler the scowler the sledgehammer
fade in the long streets
to lives of anonymity
because everyone knows al's shanty
gives the best shoeshine in the bronx
but nobody's heard of the sledgehammer robber
nor his smiling sidekick
but maybe if he had said please
maybe
if it weren't for that sledgehammer
he might have gotten some money
free money just for being down and out and telling
some tale of rotten luck but he didn't
maybe he should have tried the pawnbroker
it was a decent sledgehammer
really
quite formidable

the spectacle

they came to see us bleed
we fought like friends
i was bigger and he stronger
so many people gathered one summer sunday afternoon
to watch two kids fight
and blur eyed i saw a man
offer him a toy pistol to beat in my brains with
but he didn't take it
he was above them
a hundred bored people
and we became an event
i could've been watching from my own window
like the great cockfight bust or a minor riot
o blessed and peaceful is the vicarious
yes yes we are the subjects of a wordsworthian poem
i'll bet there are even lakes somewhere
beyond the cloud capped tenements
and if we had some money
we might see some beauty in this too
but we'll crawl out of this half blind
and half dead and our consolation
will be to know there are those worse off
like that highland lass reaping and singing
melancholy and plaintive forever
except now poetry doesn't rhyme
and she harvests subminimum wages
while the molds fill with plastic and metal
in a third world toy factory
where no vote counts but the right one
or the left one and no union strikes
so we gather our leeches where we may and sell them
we make bets on children's fights
and stake our bucks on the rooster's razored claws
and we long for our brief childhood perhaps
if it were not so terrible

the cockfight bust

police barricade the entire street
squad cars detective cars a police bus
spectators everywhere
like celebrity seekers at a broadway opening in some old movie
and down the police lined path
prisoners are herded to meatmarket justice
booked and sentenced
to live their lives in anonymous apartments
to fatten and die in the bronx
but judicious wheels turn slowly
it takes a very long restless time
for two patrol wagons to return and reload
return and reload again and again
everyone gets bored amid all the excitement
so cops run round the corner to roundup strays
escaping through canyons of basements
and catch no one to the crowd's delight
while i count seventy eight men and women
with blankets and picnic baskets
children and babies
parading out to our applause
they wave and cheer back in temporary fame
everyone is happy as when the circus comes
to the puerto rico theater if not happier
because we are all on the stage of a great dramatic irony
and know from the corners of our eyes
that just down the street el lobo sweeps
the sidewalk he don't know nothing
he's just the janitor here
but damn those are his best fighters
hauled off in the unmarked car
while the bull in charge stands
proud as the cock of the walk
and tomorrow at dawn roosters again will crow
will they betray him he wonders
and who got the money

logic

people wonder why i curse so much
and act obnoxious and do everything i can
to keep the blessed human race off my damn back
me who was brought up to be a nice kid
by a nice italian mother and a nice castilian father
taught to speak nicely and to respect others
and elders and all god's creatures and all that crap
like the cat i befriended for ten minutes
and i don't like cats them being sneaky and all
until some stone throwing kids killed it
me who learned in junior high school
while the elders were not watching
or saw only the past or pretended not to notice
when some gang walked into math class
while the teacher was discussing the history of infinity
with academically advanced seventh graders
and beat up a girl who helped grade papers and left
the teacher did not move from his desk
and no counselor came to counsel us
and no principal stopped by to smile and to say
what an unfortunate incident this was and to lie
that this would never happen again it was just
business as usual at arturo toscanini junior high
where gangs chased intellectuals and jews
and anyone else they did not like
and the social studies teacher taught
what a great melting pot america was
when she wasn't at the police station filing assault reports
and with every punch and with every bruise
and with every broken year of my youth i learned
that the more i cursed the less i fought
and the less i fought the less i got beat up
and the less i got beat up the better i looked
in this land of ugliness and that logic of course is power
the power to subdue a curious mind
the power to bully a loving heart

the great american motorcycle boots

black leather
red white and blue paisley inlaid
pointed toes
two american eagles stare me in the face
mean beaked and feisty eyed
all trimmed in neat white stitchery
these are the great american motorcycle boots
and this is the best of all possible ghettos
soon the city will hammer
sheet metal painted with white windows
red and blue curtains
to beautify the abandoned tenements
but the junkies are too stoned to notice
and tourists do not come here
the crazy puerto rican my uncle calls him
just a quiet guy on a loud bike
lean jeans greased hair and a slick jacket
everyone is categorized
johnny the jew who sells shoes on sundays
and slumlords on the side
the dumb guinea bookie
but we ain't hit big yet
the shanty irish cop
who may or may not pay for our honest labor
we shine their shoes with a smile
we hate each other and we love each other
better than we do the government
of this america where only the rich are free
and we are too poor to afford justice
and the loony dude speeds off on his harley
he tips big and his boots beam
bright as an immigrant's smile at the statue of liberty
red blood white eyes blue bruises
the flag won't mean a thing
when the police beat him senseless in the alley

democracy

it was decided by the noisier of the people who are delegated such powers by those who just don't give a damn that america was not such a bad place after all it being july and who needs heat or hot water in this weather anyway and at night when everyone is out the tenements don't look quite so bad and who sees them in the daytime when everyone is sleeping away the heat and the war was good for the economy reducing unemployment by sending the men to war and creating jobs for the women who could work for the guys who did not go to war and who were making big bucks and the underground economy was providing enough luxury items to go round and so it was decided by the noisier of the people who are delegated such powers by those who just don't give a damn that america was not such a bad place after all to celebrate by doing what would have been done anyway as it had become a tradition for the fourth of july so each side sent out its scouts to chinatown and little italy to gather up as much firepower as could be bought or stolen and to smuggle it and stockpile it and to distribute it at just the right time which was sunset on the fourth of july when it was decided by the noisier of the people who are delegated such powers by those who just don't give a damn that america was not such a bad place after all to celebrate by doing what would have been done anyway as it had become a tradition and so the two armies of teenagers too young for draft cards or too mean by means of their criminal records for military service assumed positions on their respective rooftops the ruddy irish above their red bricked tenements and the swarthy puerto ricans and leftover italians above their brown bricked tenements and it was decided by the noisier of the people who are delegated such powers by those who just don't give a damn that america was not such a bad place after all to celebrate by doing what would have been done anyway as it had become a tradition that the war at home had begun which was signaled by a single rocket's red glare which began the shooting of bottle rockets and m-80s and strings of firecrackers and sizzlers which went on for hour after hour keeping the old ladies and babies awake and driving the dogs crazy they cowered in corners like shellshocked veterans though casualties were light as the street was wide and nothing more than a sputtering rocket ever hit the other side mostly everything landed in the street which was by mutual decision a free fire zone and anyone or anything in it an enemy to both sides and mostly there was no one in it except a few unfortunate passersby unaware of this great fourth of july tradition and a line of parked cars which would be pockmarked by morning when the sidewalks were covered with red white and blue paper and the air reeked of sulfur and it was decided that everyone should cease fire and get some chow and shuteye and rest up for the night when it was decided by the noisier of the people who are delegated such powers by those who just don't give a damn that america was not such a bad place after all to celebrate by doing what would have been done anyway as it had become a tradition and the sun went up and down on the ceasefire and the irish and the puerto ricans and the leftover italian guys and their girls and their mothers and fathers and sisters and brothers got back out on our street to hang out to rock babies to gamble to play loud music to drink to gossip to party and to wait to wait to wait for a job for a baby for a draft notice which had become a tradition in not such a bad place after all

they told me not to sing

they told me not to sing
it was sixth grade and all the little puppets
with the sweet little children voices
in the disney exhibit were singing
it's a small world at the world's fair
where they who were not warring or starving
or working paid to stand hours together
on line to see fire dancers and the wonders
of the future like slick cars and clean
nuclear energy
communist china wasn't there because it wasn't
a country but it had the bomb
at the vatican exhibit the sistine chapel and the pietà
god and man forever reaching
the son of god dead in his mother's arms
and we were taught to sing in a castle of a school
collegiate gothic architecture to be exact
with a raised stone basement and a tall grate
upon a concrete moat to keep out the world
william lloyd garrison elementary
the great abolitionist but we were not free
from american values
learn much work hard for the corporation
pay taxes to support the war
buy records and toy machine guns
public school 31
where the teacher took away my tomtom
because i could not carry a beat
but they let me be a dead indian in the play
because i died well
or maybe they were just being kind
i lost so many fights my uncle called me canvasback
but i didn't cry and they told me not to sing
and there was nothing to sing about
where stray dogs tried to sneak into the cafeteria

for a great society lunch
i was door monitor a demotion from safety patrol
a fat kid beneath the central tower's tudor arches
mom did not want me to cross the street anyway
so they took that white plastic sash and shiny silver badge
and gave me door duty
i once admitted a mangy scrawny mutt too kind
to slam the door on its tail and the lunchroom went nuts
crazier than when some kid ate a gefüllte sandwich
i liked the gefüllte fish eaters
i figured they saved me from a lot of fights
because bullies can't beat everyone up all the time
like we could bomb cambodia but not china
and at recess we played the jets and the sharks
without the singing in the west bronx
and without the suicides
we didn't have to kill ourselves
too many others wanted to
and we lived on television dreams
but we did it the american way
tossed a coin to see which class was the sharks
then the fifth and sixth grades got it on
with fists and belts and sticks
ethnicity did not matter
just violence
and the blacks and the puerto ricans and the jews
fought like an italian gang until the bell
rang and we had to pretend to be nice
to each other and to the teacher
who made us sing but not me
because the hand raisers raised their hands
he's flat they said *we can't sing*
because of him and it was always my fault
the flat songs the lost ball games the war
the kennedy assassination the lost dreams

all my fault and she agreed and said
why don't you mouth the words for a while
and i sat through the dumb songs
like a goldfish mouthing through rainbow colored gravel
and the art teacher removed the bowling alley
from my construction paper dream house
but what did she know about my dreams
commuting to the suburbs
only in xanadu is pleasure art
and i took to the treeless streets
mouthing words for years for life
hoping to remain invisible

the malthusian theory

like every long shot it seemed like a sure shot and his legs were so long his stride so swift his torso so lean his need so great he scooped up the stakes from the 534 east 138th street crapshoot and the race was on four lucky gamblers in pursuit what do the losers care who gets the money but it was their game too and it was once their money and what else was there to do now that the game was over and the beer upset so as he passed 530 east 138th street they took after him too he led by ten yards with eight lucky and unlucky gamblers after him and their friends took notice because what else was going on to take notice of so by 526 east 138th street he was twelve yards ahead and eight gamblers and eight lucky and unlucky but otherwise bored friends were hounding him and by 522 east 138th street sixteen acquaintances of theirs must have thought how can he do that to our acquaintances because they took off too while asking each other what did he do anyway and he was sprinting in fine form with thirty two gamblers friends and lucky or unlucky but no longer bored acquaintances huffing and puffing and shouting and screaming which got everybody's attention so by 518 east 138th street thirty two pedestrians took up jogging after him and at 514 east 138th street he was still about five yards ahead of sixty four gamblers friends acquaintances and lucky or unlucky but very excited pedestrians which got the attention of the official 138th street spectators who watch everything and see nothing and sixty four of the fleetest official spectators joined the mob as our part of 138th street ran out of numbers and he turned the corner while one hundred twenty eight not so fast spectators streamed out of their doorways making that two hundred fifty six gamblers friends acquaintances pedestrians and lucky or unlucky fleet or not so fleet but no longer solemn official spectators rushing onto brook avenue to be joined by two hundred fifty six brook avenue strangers making that five hundred twelve gamblers friends acquaintances pedestrians fleet or not so fleet official spectators and lucky or unlucky brook avenue strangers who were met by five hundred twelve lucky or unlucky nondescripts from the mill brook projects making that one thousand twenty four in the curious crowd only twenty four of whom could actually see who got him first or who got the money when the ambulance carried him away which only goes to prove that the hunger of a crowd for entertainment quickly exceeds society's ability to produce amusement

beyond the window

i awaken to the feeling of noise
open the window onto the mob
convinced they would get me at last
burn me like frankenstein
lynch me from a fire escape ladder
but i am fifteen and pretty invisible
and insignificant in the grand scheme of things
this is a major operation
police and people everywhere
i can see which is all that matters
and it is always so exciting
the world beyond the window
but at night in my dreams
i am the sufferers i behold
and it is always so dark
and i am always alone in the unknown
which i know so well
familiar faces chase me
through the familiar streets of childhood
i become a stranger in my own neighborhood
who cannot see his enemy
and awaken in lonely sweat
red lights circling the ceiling
everyone is running or watching
whatever happens i will not be a part
beautiful and ugly are the beholder's eyes
o how do i walk in such a crowded world
in a riot of reality without getting lost

II

nightmare off bruckner boulevard

phantom submarines long to roam
all seven seas but cannot pass
barnacled barges rusting in the channel
of waterlogged nostalgia
for the peaceful streets of wartime
unlocked doors and blackened windows
full employment and boogie woogie
their midnight crews marooned in brown water
beyond cattails and the psychiatric hospital
and the cemetery where tides
sucked coffins from their graves
so these sailors of night
roam with the rowdy street regulars
and the ghostly memories of our parents
while the moon howls at trainloads
of dreamers dragged to destiny
and the deaf school listens to the headlight highway
that crosses avenues without looking
o the horror the horror haunting the dark
where everyplace is a strange neighborhood
drowning these swimmers of shadows
and where are the cameras to tell their tales
those who search for love in the night
why are not they immortal
whose life is an everyday occurrence
these lost navigators adrift upon
the fantastic sidewalks of the landlocked bronx

webster avenue

police prowl
looking for trouble
and coffee
the pub smells warm
of hops and hormones
of wishes realized in jukebox songs
war movies bogart televised sports
all behind those friendly doors
just across the street
and beyond the sinister shadows
of the third avenue el god rest its soul
the evil one makes smiling small talk
with strangers in the night
and off the passenger bridge
from knowledge to intoxication
over the valley of meaningless journeys
onto the sidewalk where many feet have traveled
the forlorn leaps
to a headache and stumbles
for pizza the desperate flesh
afraid and hungry the soul
lonely and thirsting
the self proclaimed retired underwater demolitions expert
is tired of the abuse he says
waves a garrison belt in our faces
does not know who we are and does not care
wants to hurt others before they hurt him
so we give him a beer
let him beat us at midnight checkers
blare the music and a young woman dances
him back to life then he vanishes
bottle in hand up the avenue of vengeance
and unseen in the night
two lovers who do not know it
throw rings of woe to the wind
and grow old together

scratch park

between the future mass murderer
and the extinct tavern
a scratch of asphalt trees
benches beside railroad tracks
that station empty and the train
from here to there seldom stops
concrete chessboards where old men battle
by day by night
beer cans are pawns on checkered squares
the nobility our empty bottles
we drink in history
and drink away our dreams
waiting for dawn
and youth to pass
each tells the other
how the other has erred
and we remain friends
for a forgotten while
and lose ourselves
in what we thought would be fulfillment
empty as that silly solemn darkness
of a warm night when anything may happen
and never seems to at the time

off southern boulevard

off southern boulevard where i will not tell
we find a real dirt tire rutted road
water gullies and pebbles and trees
and we who roam the night are compelled
to subliminal quests for minor satisfaction
so we walk this country lane
because it may not exist in such a city
as this and it curves beyond the known world
not a house in sight such wilderness
surrounds us with ourselves
we step softly in darkness
the breeze blows through our bodies
suddenly trees disappear
beneath our feet is the fine rooftop gravel
of an unknown building and we overlook
the valley where graffitied subway cars sleep
we do not speak so as not to wake them and beyond
tenement eyes stare like stars each light
a distant life on the skyline but we are visible
only to ourselves and we look and look
into the darkness until we leave
to wander and to weary of the night

the dharma express

you never step into the same subway twice
everything changes but the human condition
drop your token or jump your turnstile
hop the dharma express
leave randomly if you will before the last
stop that finality which is always there
waiting for you or for someone else
it matters not so the motorman drives on
and in the end he begins again
thus the last becomes the first
and in the middle huddle
passengers in windowed boxcars
peering over the rooftops of history
or shunning the reflections of darkened windows
while the conductor indifferently
opens and closes her doors for all or for none
and the iron serpent chases its tail
snake eyes in time's great crapshoot
staring down the tunnels of night
and every gambler is surely
the master of his and of her fate

the bronx vikings

i see serpent ships
fierce eyed and grimacing prows
pregnant sails red as villages ablaze
blood and the setting sun red
a favorable wind and sturdy oarsmen
into the sunset which is our east
following the green coast
from the wasteland to warm winters
women and cattle aboard
immigrant explorers beyond the known world
hope the tidal lake karlsefni names it
i see water as blue
as never again
timber and ecstatic grapes
the bountiful beautiful land
salt marshes aswarm with birds
valleys and bluffs rolling to shore
huts are built fish caught
indians trade pelts for string and milk
more pelts less string
then a squabble and stone and iron clash
freydis bares herself
slaps a sword to her breast
like a berserk goddess and the battle halts

the terror of europe retreats to the waves
leaving an ax and runes for the dead
sailing to cold riches lest history repeat
and the warriors celebrate
beneath the bronx sky by the ominous sea

jonas

beyond the ocean
up the crooked strait
past hell gate
and little hell gate
and the kill
where the mainland of hill and marsh
butts the swirling tides
seven miles from civilization
and the muskets of new amsterdam
you buy land from sachem
and rent to sharecropper
so you have come mister bronck
to make a home
on the edge of the chaos of nature
where streams wind through uncleared wilderness
emmaus you call it
and there are trials and revelations
and wars
and patriotic native americans
burn farmhouses to the green green ground
and the land named after the river
that bears your name spits you out
and the land passes away
to morris and his heirs
o you should see what is left of their tombstones
fading in saint ann's churchyard
in a valley of charred bronx tenements

gouverneur morris laughs from his grave

I

gouverneur morris laughs from his grave
sunday congas are distant incessant thunder
enchanted streets swarm and scream
beyond the spikes which ban our flesh
the soul roams at will and the dead man roars
as when he rode reinless horses through revolutionary streets
carriage crash and wooden limb
lame armed and one legged
did the ladies love his bones to death
while he laughed

II

up the once cypressed ridge to grandmother's i go
where the past is always present
musk of soup wisp of ghost
the last trees lean like pale gravestones
in a land where fruit once grew
a harvest of hopeful tenants
to sweat to freeze in aging apartments
to walk through each other's railroad flat lives
the manorial house is another boxcar siding
subways tickle restless coffins

III

all is divine wisdom
what friendly consolation
leglessness so profusely argued
o to part with the other the amputee teased
and his son parted the manor
call the harlem the jordan he quipped

thus mott purchased his haven and the foundry fumed
in the shadows of saint ann's church morris lingers
in the promised land
where tenements rise to burn and crumble

IV

to have traveled so far
to have loved so many
to be buried in the bronx
a landmark in a lost paradise
continental congress and reign of terror
caustic wit and a taste for pleasure
the churchyard cannon has disappeared
did they steal that too
children run from the past
sticks rattle the cemetery fence

V

we too are lovers from ancient families
which prosper and impoverish and wander
celestial plan or random rambling we survive
when death loosens our limbs what land will we haunt
we who rejoice and rebel and enjoy what we may
what sardonic spirit beneath the pavement sprouts
saplings through the rubble of razed streets
grandfather's corpse grinned at the priest who said his eulogy
is it life or is it death that is absurd
those drums those drums those hysterical dead skins

beyond the crying tenements

sometimes moments of great beauty
minor memories of lives never lived slip
through venetian blinds to revive
wallpaper flowers in late sun
linoleum fresh as the lawn
of a great manor on a spring evening
such sweet shade before sunset
a hint of long lost dew
the sweat of creation
in this rent controlled apartment which
my ancestors painted and died

i am too young to worry
i have not been born
but float with the spirits
through trees morris planted
an immigrant arboretum
beyond the crying tenements
the avenue has drowned
the brook flows from the valley
where my lost body walks
like the incarnation of a forgotten god
in a land with no name

III

roosevelt's bust

a lean stern eyed sharp nosed
ivory fdr
dim alley window light
never open shade
railroad flat dining room
that green sofa
where nana will die
that sagging armchair
poppop supervising the yankees
black and white on the gray
long head short body
worn tube television
the table sturdy as
his smiling deathbed spirit
that maddens the priest
my cardboard circus
the crocheted lace tablecloth
sunday funnies and cereal box cutouts
my world is flat but very colorful
orphan annie and dondi
always survive

simmering spices waft
from grandmother's kitchen
she smokes her cigar
she watches the stove
talks to dad alone
incomprehensible castilian
the tin ceiling yellow as chicken skin
soup slowly cooking
an aroma so divine
even statues hunger
mom roots and razzes
bronx cheers
italian damnations

spanish rhythms
grandfather's laughter
such intonations of love
and baseball are universal
only god and government
and grandma's recipe
for wonder remain
eternal mysteries

grand and great
grandchildren live in their photographs
the yanks win and lose
mantle's knees bandaged
his bat healthy
the enameled pig smiles
a ceramic bellyful of thimbles
saved string and tomato pincushions
sideboard drawers of needlepoint and thread
arthritis stopped her stitchery
before i could remember
my elephants parade
amid clowns and acrobats
my awkward hands
topple ladies from white horses
while roosevelt
in honor atop
the parakeet and flower
embroidered doily
armlessly embraces history
on the knickknack buffet

the windup clock
ticks away the present
amid depression blue ashtrays

what a time it was
before i was born
in the beautiful bronx
pristine tenements
beflowered parks
free glassware at five cent
double feature movies
five cent trolleys
through well swept cobblestones
everything cost the nickel
no one had
neighbors thinned the stew
and shared
all night unlocked doors
at christmas santa left
love and best wishes
nothing to fear but hunger
and fascism

spreading across the old countries
new boots for new soldiers
new slogans new marches new weapons
ancient carnage
busby berkeley musicals
movietone news
austria ethiopia
guernica manchuria
a distant world looms
this nation of immigrants
will row row row
with roosevelt across oceans
of unforeseen future
what rendezvous with destiny
a generation of loyal youth
leave school to seek

honest work honest pay
cardboard fills the holes
in weary shoes which do not fit
poor feet are callused and crooked
our fathers' toes never unfurl

the full belly
is the american dream
hoovervilles
the legacy of greed
no feast will erase
memories of young hunger
the solemn inability of parents to provide
holiday lights seem distant as stars
one treeless christmas
father smashes saint nick
reindeer crumble
beneath the angry hammer
plaster dust paint chips childhood
beaten into the tablecloth
his lone protest in a lifetime of labor
tears are reserved
for the suffering of others
lindbergh's baby
the hindenburg disaster
the iron man of baseball
retires and new york grieves

gehrig's speech replays
cameras microphones
ashen faces
free dish theaters and free lunch bars
in the land of the free
in brook avenue back rooms
the bund meets

catholics jews wobblies
the roosevelts are suspect
unions rally in union square
police tail suspicious agitators
social justice may be blasphemy
against the economic pyramid
cops crack loiterers
nightsticks in broad daylight
free beer free apples free shoeshines
for the officer on the beat
city marshals evict the unfortunate
are not responsible for missing valuables
the fbi keeps files
even on eleanor

these are the good old days
so fondly remembered
strikeouts forgotten
home runs sail forever
into happy bleachers
prohibition prohibited
dutch schultz dead
all that beer and no money for drink
this nation thirsts for work
the cigar makers guild
extinguished by the economy
grandpa's fingers have nothing to roll
farmless families head to california
jobless men wander through cities
free rent for the first month
the desperate move often
sons return to empty apartments
and angry landlords
friendly neighbors
whisper the new way home
the family endures

gathers together
the radio warm as a hearth
never lost never sold
fireside chats
sound effect serials
yankee slugfests
the young dream the old forget
baseball transcends history
for a while and the crowds cheer
roosevelt rides triumphant through the bronx
the working poor wave to their hero
forever in the old photograph
tidy streets and stores
no gates no graffiti
aunt helen out her window
mother by the doorway
the tenements are the same
only the poverty has changed
all are immigrants and the immigrants are
fellow americans
compassion is nourished by despair

the war feeds those it does not destroy
pearl harbor bombs the consciousness
blue and gold stars hang in tenement windows
the bronx is a small part
of the great arsenal of democracy
defense contracts war bonds
ration books scrap metal drives
air raid drills in darkened streets
submarines offshore
enemy agents anywhere
loose lips sink ships
the shellshocked do not talk
sons leave sons return

if only in the dreams of mourners
wives work and wait and worry
my grandparents settle
in a railroad flat for the rest of their lives
freedom from want freedom from excess
social security working sons military paychecks
rent paid and food in the pot
the buffet fills with meager memorabilia

grandma's soup remembers
meals that could not be
eight hours eighty years to cook
potatoes gold with spice
chicken melting in broth
time melts the flesh
fingers pale and wrinkled rub
my temples when i am ill
her magic fills all emptiness
with patient love
grandpa is a quiet man
a smile holding a pipe
my circus is a gift
cereal coupons she carefully saved
he watches whitey ford
laughs at clowns between innings
i am the portly ringmaster
tigers are hungry lions roar
loud as times square on victory day
the poor and lousy umpires
are always among us

roosevelt's bust commemorates
the promise of america
the hero who does not survive

the great war he wins
korea vietnam the gimcrackery grows
the beginnings of wars never end
eliot ness chases criminals on late evening reruns
hoover hunts pacifists
spies upon kennedy and king
the invincible heroes are long dead
modern heroes are slain
in slow motion nightly news replays
we are empty of tears
roger maris is no bambino
mother knows the future
is never as good as the past
never again will i taste such soup
the future is death
the past a golden dream
pain digested fun remembered
in words in wonder in silent vision

and in dreams when i wander
through the shadows of that apartment
for one more hug one more smile
one more succulent mouthful
of youth of love
never again will i feel so safe
so afraid of those eyes staring through history
watchful as an eagle
i am what i never could imagine
i have seen america forsake the forgotten
feed the rich starve the poor
people die people die
but no man may abolish memory
no hellfire may kill
human consciousness
the blue ashtrays sit

in mother's kitchen
i have grown i have gone
the embroidery will be given
to my children when i die
and the words i forge with mortal hands

nana held my hand
so tightly her fingers seemed young
she lay on the avocado herringbone couch
rolled over and died the next day
poppop months later in lincoln hospital
rolling his eyes while priest
and pentecostal vied for his soul
the priest fed his ears
the pentecostal filled his belly
in hungry times
death won and he smiled
the yankees lost but we did not care
closets of yellowed magazines
cupboards of dishes but no one was hungry
knickknacks and photographs
lifetimes of possessions scattered and gone
my circus lost in the tears of adolescence
in my grandparents' apartment
amid cheers and feasts
and the fragrance of nostalgia
roosevelt's lost bust stares like remembered love

IV

saint mary's park

fuzzy caterpillars

don't play with fuzzy caterpillars
warns the old woman
black hat black dress
wrinkled cheeks drooping brow
she does not sweat
in the summer sun
she knits
she looks us in the eye
never misses a stitch
never misses an eye
she sits
at the entrance to everywhere
the tenement stoop
the grocery
the park
huddled on a bench
the promenade beneath the flag
where once flowers grew
you'll get pimples
you play with fuzzy caterpillars
we nod politely
she says nothing more
our mothers say hello
and that is all
she smiles
and that is all
we laugh inside
three cousins young with summer
she smiles she knows
we don't give a damn about pimples
or old women
this is america

not the old country
we are three cousins young with summer
what does anyone older than ten
know about anything
we play on fields worn
by scrimmage and baseball
rocks erode with the climbing
we gather catalpa pods
in sacrificial piles
tear them and scatter the seeds
which will not grow for the mowing
we chase each other through wooded paths
reenacting television manhunts
and play with the fuzzy caterpillars
walking them on sticks and fingers
saint mary's park
is a world beyond the immediate
we are immortal
for a while
beyond maroon bricked buildings
with treeless courtyards
and streets amuck with screaming youth
here there are no consequences
to actions
we do not reap what we sow
heroes and villains reincarnate
teams win forever
to invisible cheers
glory and great parks
are fruits of the imagination
there is nothing to fear
but dinner time
on the third day we awaken
to pimples
red bellies pink thighs

which fade quicker than memory
even our mothers are surprised
butterflies scare us more than bees
was it the fuzz
or the caterpillar
or a moth's lesson
we wonder
but not for long
we take stones
and destroy anthills
you'll make it rain
if you kill ants
mother warns
but we know that mud
drives night crawlers from their holes
and what are worms but catalpa pods
with wiggle and blood
slime sometimes
but no fuzz
the sun is a rash
in the graying sky
the old woman knits
the needles crackle
like lightning
at the entrance
to thunder

lost playgrounds

the small playground is nearly empty
our mothers worry as they chat
the longtime sisters
remember moonlight dances
the band in the gazebo
twilight softball games
on diamonds where now gamblers play
fenced gardens
no walking on the grass
irish police with billy clubs
protecting flowers from italians
the rules are quite lax now
at night the park is a wilderness
more frightening than dreams
solitude is unsafe as a mob
we are herded to the main playground
a frenzy of children
shriek in the sprinkler
sing on swings
bicker on see saws
hoot on monkey bars
in the courts beyond
retired italians play boccie
we are lost in play
our mothers lost in gossip
the boccie players lost
in memories of the old days
the polish lady
lost in her knitting
the caterpillars
lost in metamorphosis
the catalpa seeds lost
in america's machinery
somewhere our fathers
are lost in work

they are quiet men
who have forgotten how to scream
lost to them
the summer afternoons
they sweat to give us
the hot sun
the cool water
the rainbow sensations
of young flesh
the growing hunger
we do not yet realize

the seasons before

the fall sun is low
the shadows long
late sunday afternoon
the churches are closed
nana's soup
waits in the pot
i walk with my father
flat feet
trench coat
brimmed hat
like a television detective
a stereotype
he never denied
not bad for a bank clerk
the wind blows
through reddening maples
the seasons before computers
replace brains
and drugsters chase
the last kids from the park
before semiautomatic teens
prowl the hopelessness that is america
four youths wielding
broomsticks and a bowling pin
emerge from the sunset
i am too young to be afraid
and dad too old
that's a nice bowling pin
i say to no one
that's a nice bowling pin
dad says to the big one
the kid hands it to him
they run off into the twilight
red and white and scratched
i set it as the centerpiece

of grandma's table
luscious as her stew
it remains in my room
my favorite trophy
of the long ago time when
we are father and son together
on a field in the bronx highlands
strong and cool as
the autumn wind
the seasons before i learn
we are not immortal

rosebud

down dead man's hill
on a washing machine cover
white enamel
white snow
slick as
white lightning
i lose my mind
in december air
or is it my body
i feel light
as a snowflake
tiny and distant as stars
dad waits
at the bottom of the hill
no i cannot keep
the sleek square
this white rosebud
must remain a gift
to some humble child
who has not planned
on ecstasy
and speeds down the ridge
like a meteor
to land in the bronx
and rise again
the spontaneity of fun
amid the desperate tenements
father waits patiently
i brush snow
off sunday pants
we had not expected
this wandering
we walk home
in quiet darkness
together in the cold

flesh and blood

we climb the approach to janes' hill
his mansion lost
the foundry forgotten
how wondrous to live among the trees
to cast iron for the world
the capitol dome
the savannah fountain
to sell dragons and lions to china
and live unafraid above mott's haven
when parks were unnecessary
the slope is a cowboy movie mountain
i never knew
my father could climb rocks
never knew
i could climb anything
i follow his fingers
holding narrow crevices
too amazed to be afraid
he does all this
wearing a sports jacket and dress shoes
there is no work today
he must have been some kid
heroes never brag about the past
don't say much about the present
at the top we stand like warriors
waiting for a dream vision
the sky is blue beyond
the clouds which roll to the eastern sea
my father is a man of flesh and blood
a modest life a modest death
the bronx grass growing green
over fields and graves
he is the man who made me
the man who gives me life

the trees of saint mary's

buildings die and factories leave
the neighborhood moves
to yonkers or jersey
new neighborhoods arrive
move in move on
across seas and streets
humans flit to certain futures
bronx boulevards lead
to mainland usa
farms platted and wilderness farmed
history is an unremembered
flowerless cemetery
the present is suburban sitcom
its poverty subliminal
this park is the lingering wealth
of an ancient earth
even street signs are mortal
discarded is the decorum
of enamel letters in curved frames
lost the love of here
the elegance of street and avenue
historic names on reflective rectangles
are vestiges of the forgotten
lost are the tales of those who came before
dead the carvers of roads through the wilderness
dead the weckquasgeeks the siwanoy
their long houses long buried
saint ann's churchyard
the last remains of morris manor
the subway station's tile initials
a mere hint of mott haven
art nouveau street lamps
ornate traffic signals
vanished with the cobblestones
mercury lamps glow

like sullen moons
lightpoles are the bare and modern
blighted forests of urban childhood
the past is lost
the future is sold
the trees of saint mary's
are sad as mothers
who have lost their sons
i too will grow away
the trees have roots
sturdier than housing projects
older than tenements
their limbs are prayers on the wind
there is comfort in
those open arms

fires and evictions
redevelopment and decay
seasons of brick and rubble
mother raises me
in the apartment where her parents died
these are the sturdy limbed trees
she knew as a child
she shares them with me
we sit on a bench
of concrete and wood
carvings of long ago romance
submerged in paint
amid splinters
of new love
here retirees rest from long labor
beside shopping bags
of wool and pigeon feed

and bottle babies gurgle
from rocking strollers
breastfeeding has vanished
in the civil rights era
this year's leaves
are green with july
the sky hot with noon
the main concourse
of saint mary's park
on the cypress ridge
in the shade
the same sun
the same trees
the same shade
she walked as a girl with her father

he loved to walk
she loves to walk
i love the trees
the depth of their darkness in the light
i love to walk
through the bronx as she knew it
the ice cream cart
has jingle bells
is christmas in summer
to young mouths
she buys me
what she could not have
when she sunday strolled
through the great depression
with her father
his youngest hope
his little charmer

there were puppet shows
and outdoor movies
no sound
but birds and crickets
the bond of child
and parent never forgotten
the thrill of evening breeze
on the rocks of dead man's hill
they sat together
the wonders of america
flickered before innocent eyes
cowboys villains cops crooks
heroes got their men
ladies kissed their heroes
america seemed orderly
as the circling stars
cobblestones glowed like broadway
and on the walk home
the apartment lights
sparkled with hope
there will be work
there will be food
immigrant streets safe
as the old country
the apartment is crowded with sleep
imagine what shadows
the trees cast in moonlight

i am her only child
in a changing world
she cannot give me
the freedom of her childhood
there are no trolley tracks

to follow to the palisades
no fish in the polluted waters
children who wander
may never return
this is the age
of guns and butter
the rich have the butter
the poor have the guns
death in the jungles
death on the streets
in the age of prosperity
hope erupts to despair
beyond the reach of our hands
the squirrel eats peanuts
his wariness is rhythmic
two bites and a glance
two bites and a glance
presidents and ministers
are not safe in america
two glances and on to the next nut
there are nuts everywhere
mother says
but here the sky is blue and the shade is cool
the benches are lined with drowsy mothers
old women knit winter sweaters
old men throw seed to the birds
they smile like benevolent kings
throwing coin to peasants
startled by a toddler's enthusiasm
the squirrel scurries for the safety of the trees

time stops sometimes on summer afternoons
conversation blurs in the heat

distant as the whine of cicada
the rustle of breeze
and through the invisible doorway we emerge
beyond history and abstraction
to the body and blood
we are
parent and child
forever connected
forever safe
in this womb of trees
floating in a surf of sky
a baby cries and we
are ourselves
who is this woman
who loves me
who will not let me out of her sight
until the waves of seasons
push me into the world
what does she think
pushing me ceaselessly on swings
does she wonder when
i will fly away
does she walk
again through her youth
roaming the bronx with her brothers
does she stroll arm in arm
with father through their long courtship
or simply contemplate dinner
this is the first playground
of the bronx its asphalt skin
is cracked and gray
children are busy
with childhood
there is nothing but this moment
of fun

here the poor forget hunger
here the meek are not afraid
here the sad are lost in laughter
the innocent times before gangs
graffiti the rocks
before the sun is malignant
and the moon a mere golf course
there is nothing but
the exhilaration of life
gravity cannot hold us
we are seeds on the wind
sent forth from timeless trees
the falling from youth
seems eternal
the flight of maple wings
the plunge of acorn and pod
we land in the green world of infinite summer
the trees will not grow old
the trees will keep us forever safe
in the shade of knowledge and life
saint mary's park is heaven on earth
hell is the streets where we suffer and die

V

pastoral esplanades

pastoral esplanades were the streets where we played
o the hills o the dales o happily
bleating we lamb gamboled
the concrete pastures of the beautiful bronx

woolly wild we ran and feared no fate
frenzied frivolous too young to be damned
though pedestrians panicked and cursed
death's shepherd would not fleece us

and glorious the metermen jingled and glorious the metermaids sang
in metered bush beneath steel bough of streetlight
echoing with sylvan joy the festive tenements
where dionysian oracles staggered and moaned

o did shopping bag ladies murmur melancholy strains
o were fire escapes ancient pathways to olympus
over the lofty rooftops jets droned like warring titans
and promethean tears rained upon the caucasian skyline

in the lush of this asphalt arcady did we leap
amuck with wonder and joy at the lovely world
we will never grow old we will never grow weary
of sailing the winds of summer never

behold the triborough bridge sleeping
like cerberus across the hell gate

ferry point park

we may turn our backs
on housing project and cemetery
pretend to see the ocean
beyond gulls cawing over the sound
really the restless east river
which ebbs and flows whirling with tides
from sunrise to hell gate
but the horizon is the whitestone bridge
a turquoise arch suspended overhead
vibrant with hum of car and truck and seabound wind
there are no white stones
no ferries
dad and i fished here once
no fish
just empty fields and a busy bridge
and waves to tangle bait amid the boulders
that prop up a land of landfills
and buttress the buttresses of a long road
which crosses even the sky
to the green suburban shores
of queens beyond unswimmable waters
and westchester creek
its half sunk rusted barge
aglow and unmoving in the bronx sun
temporarily triumphant
in its long war with eternity
while we forget the lives which keep us apart
and stand together father and son
new york's skyline lost in the southwest haze
strangely alone and strangely united
in the awkward peace which blows
just beyond our daily world
with nothing to say and no need to speak
on the shore of the land of our birth
beyond a sea of ancestors

one to die here one to leave
but we do not think of the future
and a narrow strip of beach amid the rocks
where footprints wash away
and that bridge
with the promise of there being someplace to go
and the clouds
and a sky towering over the towers
with the promise of heaven

the subway grating fisherman

i am a subway grating fisherman
everything i can imagine is down there
slightly below the sidewalk
in subterranean gills
slightly out of reach
beneath steel waves
on the cement shores of the abyss
of eternal boredom
such is youth
a stringed magnet
the glisten of hope in the sludge
to be caught by a patient hand
and desperate faith in the renewal
of the familiar
let the big boys fish
with hot bubble gum or cold vaseline
for what coin falls from the rich
i haul in the bottle caps
which no one wants
so beautifully
ordinary

maples forever

i hope the maples are still there
and the wading pool and monkey bars
the little playground off brook avenue
leafy maples that hide alleys and backyards
the gray windows of sweaty kitchens
curtained bedrooms for the weary to rest
and shade the sandbox and the sidewalk checkerboard
thirteen squares the center is dead man's land
we shoot bottle caps from number to number
a game of skully beneath rustling leaves

beyond the branches are schools
that teach how not to be young
industry feeds educated workers
the american dream not dreaming artists
what we draw in chalk will wash away
fantasies fade in the fluorescence of technology
money is real the sky but a blue
emptiness of untouchable clouds
and a drizzle of maple pods spiraling down
slow and steady and fruitless upon the asphalt

future forests blowing away
like the wonders of childhood

crossing invisible streams

school teaches all a nuclear man must know
montgomery
vietnam
purple mountains
bloody plains
but this land is mystery
submerged in sidewalk
the forgotten earth
the stream of smooth stones
mosholu mosholu
it babbles off the tongue
mosholu mosholu
stream of smooth stones
native americans named it
and vanished like the water
street signs mock the history beneath our feet
hills hidden by tenements
invisible streams trapped in sewers
mortar and brick
cement and stone
the landscape is a mutation of the inanimate
mosholu parkway the reality we know so well
parkway parkway
mowed grass embanks the asphalt
the tarmac is a free fire zone
where they wait to break our bones
they who are not at war overseas
ready to run their cars over our sneakers
to shove us with their bumpers
just for laughs
they will catch reruns of lucy
before the nightly news
they have color televisions
better to see the blood with
jungle blood street blood

black and white and yellow
the blood is red
redder than lucy's hair
the real world is bloodier
than john wayne movies
we gather to charge
like hollywood indians we yell
but we do not cry
we will survive
eight thousand boys
dewitt clinton high school's
wary students learning america
the largest boys' school short of the army
there are no green lights
no negotiations
no plans but instinct
this is the war of generations
and we have come to do battle
where the lost stream runs
invisible as innocence
it begins with a few bold scouts
a spearhead of impromptu volunteers
then we swarm the cars
no one says let's go
we just do
a battalion of boys who simply want to go home
dodging impatient commuters
grandmothers in mustangs who seek revenge
on wayward youth
housewives out for a few thrills
businessmen too busy to join the war
o how they love the action
but they can't bash all of us all the time
we will survive
we ford the highway

the city lies ahead
safety is in the herd and we stampede the trail
through mosholu park
a few trees mowed grass an old name
benches where veterans
play chess and handicap horses
here traitors ambush us
a barrage of stones and pennies
we are many and desperate
they are few and they flee
we overrun the wall
up the ancient el station's stairs
to fall is perilous
our feet are young
we hurl our momentum
at gates and turnstiles
surly cops with clubs and guns
check subway passes
cull those to search
for weapons and draft cards
most of us are deemed
only old enough for football
the army may want us someday
but the conductor does not
he closes electronic doors on our mortal necks
while our buddies help us aboard
all we have is each other
we pack into the train
restless and weary and rowdy as soldiers on leave
deploying to tenements and projects
warm girl friends and minimum wage jobs
the rails cross the bronx skyline
steel stanchions rooted
in the stream that became jerome avenue
the woodlawn train begins at the cemetery

and disappears into the ground
woodlawn woodlawn
trees and tombstones on the lawns of death
war memorials remember the fallen
do the dead learn
the secrets of the land beneath the asphalt
do they wander
the lost paradise of the bronx
there will be new wars
there will be new warriors
the tunnel leads to wall street
the heart of america
like our parents we are
ceaseless commuters
carried by unrelenting wheels
we too love the dauntless lucy
and admire the streamlined cars
that race through the commercials
which fund the nightly news
where officers of the peace
beat peaceful demonstrators
and the war continues to bring peace to vietnam
police bleed
protesters bleed
soldiers bleed
civilians bleed
but most endure
we watch the blood
we await our futures
alone in hopeful fear
we are young warriors wandering
the asphalt concrete wilderness
we are young warriors crossing
invisible streams to survive

saint jude's bazaar

money comes and goes but gimcrackery is forever
we toss coins on lucky numbers
we are nickel and dime gamblers
on the great wheel of fortune
hopelessly lost in ordinary lives
in toil and worry
in the ebb and flow of currency
summers of sweat
cold tenement winters
days of work nights of dreams
life must be better
in the suburbs we watch on television
the suburbs which are always
just beyond the next river
we have crossed the harlem
but we have not been transformed
we seek the impossible but savor trifles
we have passed through the darkness
into a place of noise and light
the church is empty
the basement smells of sawdust and beer
it's las vegas night the local parishioners
pray to beat the house
they win they lose they cycle
through various heavens and hells and emerge
happy to be on earth
only mildly hung over
only moderately broke
they join us in the playground carnival
here pocket change can become
tangible trophies of good fortune
here the game tents are full
of plastic toys of plaster lamps
radios ashtrays stuffed animals
pen knives and cigarette lighters

and the wheels spin
and the wheels spin
the ferris wheel turns and turns
cotton candy winds out of sticky machines
people walk round and round
shedding money as they go
summer is spinning away
autumn nights are long and cool
that geisha lamp will brighten them
that stuffed bear will bring warmth
when the furnace is broken when the super is drunk
when the landlord did not pay the fuel bill and there is no heat
and in the midwinter darkness i will see it again
see it as i do each year at the ten o'clock raffle
a heavenly vision over upturned faces
the crowd silent the ferris wheel still
passengers swaying in the starless haze
the tickets are turned in a clear rotisserie
rising and falling and rising again
hope burns in the night
the adults look grim but the children
grasp the impossible
the children whose imaginations are more vivid
than the sticky asphalt crowded
with the odds that are against them
the priest slowly climbs the steps
the priest bares his innocent arm
the priest unlocks the door to eternal childhood
and raises the chosen one to the sky
from above a voice pronounces the numbers
the winner comes forth to fulfill
the dreams of the multitude
white stubs rain down from losing hands
there is nothing to do but return to the bronx
and i will see it again and again

when i am old and my knees are bad and my hair is falling out
the big red bicycle
a made in america schwinn
hand brakes
gears to shift
on this i will ride
through an imaginary childhood
down tree lined streets
neighbors will smile and wave
i will have friends and we
will fish and play baseball
in little league teams with uniforms
and ride our bicycles home for lunch
and year after year we make the pilgrimage
to saint jude's bazaar
and the big red bicycle raffle
one dollar a ticket but i never win
and year by year i realize
how foolish it would be
to ride this bicycle through the bronx
dodging trucks and bicycle bandits
and i have no friends to protect me
father wins a car
uncle hits the number and buys a mustang
but we never leave the bronx
we always return to the treeless streets
the tenement has not been incinerated
the apartment has not been burglarized
when we turn on the lights
the roaches make a polite exit
and life is as beautiful
as it would be anywhere
there is food in the refrigerator
there is love at the table
and i have not been killed

defending my big red bicycle from street gangs
in my room the calcium paint has chipped
white craters float like clouds
and the streetlight shines like the moon
at dawn heat rises through the radiators
hot water flows through the pipes
teddy bear has gone
to teddy bear heaven
the exotic lamps are hooked
to automatic timers to fool burglars
i follow the american dream
i work hard buy a house and a rusting chevy
i play the state lottery
the odds look good to a poet
at sunrise i walk to stretch the stiffness from my joints
my number has not come up
and i believe in miracles
they are everywhere
in the hope
in the suffering
in the fluttering emptiness of the suburban morning

Bibliography: Previous Publications {concrete pastures of the beautiful bronx}

beyond the window: *Dusty Dog.* June, 1991.

the bronx vikings: *POETS <u>on the line</u>.* No. 3, spring 1996.

the cockfight bust: *Turnstile.* Vol. III, no. 2, 1992.
I didn't know there were latinos in Wisconsin. Focus Communications. 1999.

democracy: *A Multicultural Reader: Collection Two.* Perfection Learning Company. 2002.
I didn't know there were latinos in Wisconsin. Focus Communications. 1999.
Welcome to Your Life: Writings for the Heart of Young America. Milkweed Editions. 1998.
Two Worlds Walking: Short Stories, Essays, & Poetry by Writers with Mixed Heritages. New Rivers Press. 1994.

the dharma express: *The Critic.* The Thomas More Association. Vol. 48, no.1, fall 1993.

the cockfight bust: *Turnstile.* Vol. III, no. 2, 1992.

ferry point park: *Connections: New York City Bridges in Poetry.* P & Q Press. 2012.
North Coast Review. Issue 7, 1995.

jonas: *The Bronx County Historical Society Journal.* Vol. XLV, nos. 1 & 2, spring/fall 2008.
POETS <u>on the line</u>. No. 3, spring 1996.

logic (selected lines): *Bronx Accent: A Literary and Pictorial History of the Bronx.* Rutgers University Press. 2000.

logic: *Dusty Dog.* Vol. 2, no. 1, January 1991.

the malthusian theory: *The Party Train: A Collection of North American Prose Poetry.* New Rivers Press. 1996.

maples forever: *North Coast Review.* Issue 7, 1995.

nightmare off bruckner boulevard: *The Critic.* The Thomas More Association. Vol. 48, no.1, fall 1993.

off southern boulevard: *The Critic.* The Thomas More Association. Vol. 48, no.1, fall 1993.

roosevelt's bust (selected lines): *Bronx Accent: A Literary and Pictorial History of the Bronx.* Rutgers University Press. 2000.

saint mary's park (selected lines): *Bronx Accent: A Literary and Pictorial History of the Bronx.* Rutgers University Press. 2000.

scratch park: *The Critic.* The Thomas More Association. Vol. 48, no.1, fall 1993.

the spectacle: *Dusty Dog.* Additional Issue, April, 1991.

the subway grating fisherman: *The Critic.* The Thomas More Association. Vol. 48, no.1, fall 1993.

they told me not to sing: *Sometimes Anyway: Pride in Poetry Volume II.* Navworks Press. 2017.
The Critic. The Thomas More Association. Vol. 48, no.1, fall 1993.

webster avenue: *The Critic.* The Thomas More Association. Vol. 48, no.1, fall 1993.

from the banks
of brook avenue

w r rodriguez

zeugpress

Dedicated to Mike Peterson, in gratitude for his technical advice and support of my publication projects over the decades.

Acknowledgments

Poems from this book previously appeared in the following magazines and anthologies: *And Justice For All; The Bronx County Historical Society Journal; Connections: New York City Bridges in Poetry; Dusty Dog; The Glacier Stopped Here: an anthology of poems by Dane County writers; Live Lines: Is There a Place for Poetry in Your World?; North Coast Review; POETS <u>on the line</u>; The Prose Poem: An International Journal; The Spirit That Moves Us; Tokens: Contemporary Poetry of the Subway; Welcome to Your Life: Writings from the Heart of Young America; You Are Here: New York City Streets in Poetry;* and *Z Miscellaneous.* The short poem, "genghis khan," by w r rodriguez, previously appeared in *Wormwood Review.* It serves as the basis for "yankee kitchen."

Cover Photo: *Glass Clouds* by Rob Rodriguez

© 2015 w r rodriguez
All rights reserved

Printed in the United States of America

ISBN: 978-0-9632201-3-4 *(from the banks of brook avenue)*

zeugpress

Contents

I
forbidden places 7
a moon full and cold 8
just another new york city subway near death experience 10
yankee kitchen 12
the beach beneath the bridge 14
after seeing *night of the living dead* 15
on the coping 16
liberation: the brook avenue parking meter quartet 18
justice 22
she is leaving but 23
what could have more impact than a bus 24
plaza of the undented turtle 26
avenue b, 14th street, looking south 29
the push and break and chase of it 30

II
the third avenue el 33
standing upon the fordham road bridge 37
halloween 38
ne cede malis: poem for the seal of the borough of the bronx 40
washington comes to visit 42
grandfather: a photograph 43
bootblacks on the loose 44
al 46
p.s. 43 47
cypress avenue 50
skully 52
the tire man 54
a small but perfect world 56
the fountain of youth 58

III

welcome to the mainland 61
america's favorite pastime 65
yankee fan 66
the gambling leaguers 69
lost again on old subways 70
randall's island 72
triborough bridge: suspension 75
triborough bridge: stasis 76
triborough bridge: genesis 78
triborough bridge: kinesis 79
astoria park 80
from the banks of brook avenue 82

Bibliography: Previous Publications 84

I

*… a wholly new ordering
of ordinary
affairs.*

forbidden places

in all the forbidden places
like round the corner
and too far up the block
and up and down the you'll fall from it fire escape
and across the bad boy bad girl rooftops
of fertile pigeons and antenna thieves

through the sinister shadows of subway stations
and beware of dogs junkies
and the drunken super
basements
through the unexplored side streets of childhood
my mind wanders

that musk of the living
and dying tenement compels me
the gloom of alley and airshaft
the glow of sunlight on brick
i must navigate asphalt rivers
i must trek the broken glass

graffitied mainland to reach
the cement heart of the interior
and i will not return
i am the great explorer forever lost
in the concrete wilderness
i will discover america

flowering in the rubble

a moon full and cold

there was a moon full and cold
and i was a child in the big wide
unwanderable world
kept safe by my parents and warm
while the radiator with its ancient scales
of cracked paint hissed like a tame dragon

through the green forests
and brown fields of footworn linoleum
plastic soldiers advanced from their beachhead
to conquer the living room or to die in glorious battle
cowboys and indians skirmished at fort apache
alien spacecraft landed and robots ran amok

gallant knights with british accents
rode forth from castle walls to great adventure
fighting firebreathing worms and other strange creatures
so the countryside would be safe for travelers
and a child might sleep in bed and fear no harm
there was no gore just valor and victory and i

was general or prince or hero
anything is possible in the moonlight
this is the moon that shone over stalingrad
when death oozed through the rubble
this is the moon that glowed over the balcony
when romeo swore his love and juliet was enchanted

a leafless lifeless moon amid the tarpaper sky
which rose above the rooftops which shrouded our souls
shining white beyond empty streets and unlit windows
beyond unseen sleepers and reason and dream
a moon bright and distant
as a future as a friend as a life beyond the immediate

i pressed my nose to the windowpane and saw the moon
looming over lovers and battlefields
i wanted to sit forever in its light
to drink in the heavens to drown in wonder
ecstatic and enraptured
sated and thirsting for more

the fearless loveless bloodless moon
beyond the who and what and where of the sun's despair
its stark chill beckoned unanswerable

just another new york city subway near death experience

116th street and lexington avenue
three of us in the subway car
like some underground golgotha
when mister death walks in
not looking too kindly
we are not feeling immortal today
he is six feet tall he is five feet wide
he can sit anywhere he wants
but he stands right over me
cold eyes solemn mouth
in one hand a thick belt
dangles like a scythe
(the other holds the commuter strap
for proper balance because giants
do not like to tumble before their prey)
as the train rocks along
like the history of western civilization
which is irrelevant at this moment
of imminent doom
his eyes do not blink
his mouth does not smile
(i have lost my sense of humor
and all other sensation)
that immense hand
that mysterious belt
dangling in my peripheral vision
like a glimpse of heaven beyond pain
i cannot speak
i cannot run
the enormous gray clad arm
moves and the belt
taps my knee
taps my knee three times
his eyes do not move

i do not move
nor think nor feel
i have transcended
humanity in a subway tunnel beneath spanish harlem
and he walks off
to the next passenger
and taps his knee
three times then on to the next
three times and there are only three passengers
so he lumbers into the next car
searching for knees
and i feel like sir gawain released by the green knight
introspective and glad to be alive
i am young and i have learned
that experience is not unique
that the inevitable is
sometimes avoidable though i don't know how
and that for a mere fifteen cent token i can wander
forever searching for the man who taps knees
but when a voice says *shoot boy it was just another*
new york city subway near death experience
i remember that i was going to play basketball and maybe
talk to some girls afterwards though i am
a lousy shot and terribly
socially awkward

yankee kitchen

there are paintings of quaint towns by the sea
and clippers slicing windswept waters
wood trim and white bricks
a touch of new england in new york
with a whiff of chowder on the menu
harbored next to a massive gray church
where angels watch over the world
and the monstrance shines over the globe
and the winged herald on the corner wields a trumpet
louder than all the taxicabs on lexington avenue
if only we could hear it
but we sail the winds and waves of adolescence
and drift back to this modest diner
with its patina of grease and nicotine
to listen to ourselves and feast
upon just being friends
in that delicious time
before the future pulls us apart
and we become like the pedestrians beyond the window
scurrying to love to money to fashionable
restaurants or dive bars
honking like traffic at anything in the way
some of us will make the angels cry
some will just wander off
into life but for now
we have nothing to do but sit
together and sip our sodas until the ice
turns to water while ralph
the aged waiter with the patience of a saint
lean and drawn like the farmer in *american gothic*
and a loving smile pretends not to see
jerry use his straw to shoot spitballs at the good
citizens of nantucket so purposefully
portrayed in oil amid the rustic wooden frame

while in the infernal heat of the kitchen
the anonymous infamous fry cook grills
hamburgers cheeseburgers and anything we can afford
we do not know his name but we call him
genghis khan because legend has it he once
charged from the grill waving a butcher knife
at a customer who complained
so we laugh and to the last
lick of grease eat clean the bone
white plates of our hungry
youth

the beach beneath the bridge

a strip of sand and stone
between overgrown grass and gray water
white suburban homes mottle the leaves
of a distant shore
thirteen years old our footprints
are pools in the mud
we walk away
from parents and baseballs
there are mussels and driftwood
a horizon and a sky
ashes of bonfires burnt out
like the passion of night's lovers
the beach is awash with a love we barely understand
the smell of lowtide mud and brine
there is no going back not yet
the uncertain future ebbs and flows
now beneath the bronx sun we run and laugh
and stumble in the cold dark waves

after seeing *night of the living dead*

stiffarmed we limp across the commons
they're coming to get you barbara
we yell from dormitory bushes
on this hallowed ground
where edgar allan poe
once haunted the jesuits
but no one is scared so we
stagger into the pub to bend
our elbows till dawn
pretending to be
cinema heroes and poets
and in the platonic light of day
when we are only ourselves
they up and run
premeds
junior accountants
student politicians
literally up and run
they conform so well
we not at all
they will flourish and prosper
we will write and paint and teach
and grow old paying bills
starving for the days
and nights when we
roamed the gothic campus
young alive hungry
liberal arts
rebels

on the coping

atop the parapet
of a five story walk-up
on the outer edge
of coping

he stands
fifty feet in the air
upon the smooth
downward slope of tile

his kite soars
a soul
in search of heaven
and he smiles

childhood stops
children gaze
with upturned
wondering eyes

there must be angels
in the clouds
a miracle flutters
overhead

the eternity
of a summer afternoon
the immortality of youth
the timeless awe

those black sneakers
on the brink
of doom
and suddenly

a jump
a blind
backwards leap
onto the tarpaper roof

the kite
sports in the wind
and he descends
creaky stairs

to the rest of his life
to be found years later
jaundiced
needle scarred

dead in the stench
of an unlit doorway

liberation: the brook avenue parking meter quartet

I

the war droned
air america
deathdrugs
slumlord decadence
nightsticks and headblood

nor freedom from ourselves
eternities of tenements
work
sweat
survival

rentstrike
riot
petition
so many nouns and verbs
yet the poor are always among us

II

the resignation
of sun on concrete
the protest wind
of winter apartments
life is the struggle to live

brook avenue is indifferent
to saint and thief
time and space are money
taxation inevitable
and the city will take its tithe

we labor we sleep we dream
we awaken to parking meters
parking meters on brook avenue
where the sewerburied stream flows
invisible as hope

III

where orchards once grew
now stark
silver moneytrees
eat the fruit of our labor
we pay to park and we pay

for the means to make us pay
coinboxes are stolen
and we pay for replacements
by day we spend
by night we are robbed

dime by thin roosevelt dime
from weary hands
our wealth trickles
through treacherous currents
to the ocean of greed

IV

midnight's entrepreneur
is an invisible
lumberjack
hacking a trail of steel stumps
through urban wilderness

a cycle of thievery
and fruitless reforestation
meters reappear
to disappear again
and again and again

and again until
the city withdraws
from this war of attrition
no more parking meters
no more parking meter thief

the avenue is free
as a babbling brook

o liberation

justice

a youth grabbed an old woman's purse fat with tissues and aspirin and such sundries as old women carry in sagging purses a desperate youth nice enough not to beat her head bloody into the sidewalk as muggers of the feeble often do for the fun of it i suppose and he ran up the hill but one of the perennial watchers watched it all from her window the purseless old woman in slow pursuit yelling such curses as it takes old women a lifetime to learn but it was too dangerous too futile the silent watcher knew to call the police who might come and rough up someone they did not like just for the fun of it i suppose or who would talk polite and feel mad inside and roll their eyes because there was really nothing they could do and there were murders and assaults to handle so this silent angry watcher carelessly but carefully dropped flower pots from her fourth floor windowsill garden one crashing before one behind and the third hitting him on the head a geranium i suppose and closed her window while the huffing grateful old woman looked up at the heavens to thank the lord and when she finally calmed down she walked off with her purse laughing and leaving the youth to awaken in the blue arms of the law and do you know two smiling cops walked up all those stairs to warn the watcher that if she weren't more careful with her plants she would get a ticket for littering i suppose

she is leaving but

she is leaving but
pauses a moment
before the great
overhead thud
our upstairs neighbors
like to play so they wrestle
the burly father
the burly son
and the takedown
takes down the ceiling

my amazed aunt had turned to talk
stopped at the french doors
on the threshold of doom
by mundane words
a second before bricks
and whiskey bottles
left by turn of the century
italian plasterers
and genuine plaster
crash in a dusty thud

she laughs to see
a leg poking through
she laughs to be standing
in our living room
an oasis with green sofa and chair
art deco end tables and console television
she laughs just to be alive
in a rent controlled apartment
in the south bronx
where no one escapes death

and she laughs

what could have more impact than a bus

what could have more impact than a bus
boasted the bus on a bus long fluorescent sign
advertising advertising space along the roof
of this new bus and its new bus brethren
who bore the plastic banners of big corporations
making big bucks from this richest
and poorest of cities
but galloping buses are not pedestrians
to be tamed with words and money and this rare
soon to be extinct
what could have more impact than a bus bus
with a bellyful of passengers and its fluorescent plastic strip
sped past the bright shops and dark taverns
along third avenue where once
the great sad eyed el roared
and rattled tenement windows
and this rare soon to be extinct
what could have more impact than a bus bus
right outside the seventy-sixth street flophouse
where nightly floppers staggered home
amid swinging staggering singles
in the very crosswalk where daily the ancient monsignor
damn near ran out of breath while we wondered
how long he had left how many months or minutes
until he could no longer hobble to safety
before the light turned and he would be caught
in the stampede of uptown traffic and be killed
while we watched like the crowd at calvary
and did nothing to save him
we would carry the guilt to our graves
we would suffer gruesome memories
we would sweat through grisly nightmares
but he died quietly in his sleep
and the angels carried him away

and we were just streetcorner losers
with time to kill
then one day this rare soon to be extinct
what could have more impact than a bus bus
caught in mid escape a white pigeon
white as a baptismal gown white as a stained
glass window dove on a sunny sunday morning
a rare aberration of the prolific pigeons
those fellow gray loiterers
whose droppings whitewashed the steeples
of the church that spiked its windowsills
and swept up wedding rice before the flock could partake
a rare white winged apparition
caught like any of us might have been
by this rare soon to be extinct
what could have more impact than a bus bus
and it fell wide eyed
its feathers drifting slowly
spiraling white and red onto the asphalt
ground down by car after car until
even the blood disappeared
and the flying spirit disintegrated into the busy world
outside the dive bar beneath the flophouse
that will die and be reborn
in a paradise of condominiums and upscale cafes
with no room for the congregation
the aged priest may have been trying to save
with no room for elevated trains
or bored teenage boys
there was prophecy and revelation and the promise
of eternity and we knew
we too might grow old someday
if we were that lucky

plaza of the undented turtle

sirens
red lights
angry cops
the gold car speeds
down avenue
c and swerves
onto the sidewalk
through the plaza
scattering
the twelfth street midnight
beer drinkers and slams
head-on into the shell
of the beloved
cement turtle
while the skyline sparkles
postcard pretty
outside our window
ten stories above
as we watch this drama
just another city night
just another summer street
just another urban legend
seeking anonymity
reality entertains
when it happens to others and
the door flies open
the foot race begins
run driver run
from police
run police run
into the night
flow river flow
to the mysterious sea
who knows

how it ends
is there justice
on dark streets
red lights gather and vanish
gather and vanish
all life long
blood bleeds
bullets kill
the turtle
does not cry
the pontiac
has chosen to remain silent
then the impounding officer
starts the engine
it purrs it revs and it's off
to automobile prison
there is no reporter
asking the cop at the wheel
about inanimate
reincarnation
it really does
have a phoenix
painted on the hood
there is irony
to fulfill
tragedy
lust
love and laughter
babies will surface from the womb
to crawl to walk to climb
searching
for the ecstasy of heaven
now the undented turtle sleeps
beneath the electric hum

of the power plant which may
or may not explode
with a hiss and a fireball
and a boom like the big bang
as if the universe were created anew
on the lower east side
and we are lucky just to breathe
amid the smoke and the screams
and we are lucky to survive
the chaos of night
and the turtle waits for the warm sun
for the silly day for the children
to play like creatures
on the back
of the great
creator
god

avenue b, 14th street, looking south

there is a place when
there is a moment where
crossing the street
all the streetlights stretching south
and all the traffic lights
align in rows
that would converge but for
some distant building
and i think i must be
exactly in the middle
of the street but i know
the world is too crooked
for that

the push and break and chase of it

three men push a broken car down the street.
a dog chases them.

three dogs push a broken man down the street.
a car chases them.

three cars push a broken dog down the street.
a man chases them.

three men, three cars, three dogs
push each other down the street,
chase each other,
break each other.

no, no, we must not upset the order,
said the car who was really three cars who had chased the dogs.

a little innovation is in order every now and then,
said the man who was really three men who had chased the cars.

*do we not constitute a microcosm of the universal flux
from order to disorder to the establishment of a new order
to be set to chaos?*
said the dog who was really three dogs who had chased the men
and who now chased cars
following a wholly new ordering
of ordinary
affairs.

II

...our spirits drink immortal rage and compassion from the fluorescent green ooze of the waterbug writhing fountain of youth

the third avenue el

I. 1886

a bridge and shining rails span the river
the long arm of the el stretches north
from harlem through the mainland
the seeds of the bronx are sown
tenements will blossom on fertile ground
there will be streets and streetcars and immigrants

will brave the broad ocean for their chance
in the land of the free
the colossus rises above new york harbor
glorious timeless stoic
her mighty limb bears a beacon of hope
a wary welcome to the new world

where geronimo is imprisoned
where chinese laborers are expelled from seattle
where former slaves are massacred in a mississippi courthouse
no one is indicted for their murder
in this great republic where the lord
and manifest destiny work in mysterious ways

a torch a tablet a stern look
staring toward the tempestuous atlantic
the copper matron will guide
exiles to the promised land
sure footed she is stepping
in the direction of south ferry station

II. 1920

from the battery park aquarium
to the botanical gardens and beyond
all for a buffalo nickel
a stadium will be built and there will be baseball
in the bronx and babe ruth and the yankees
will come and the crowds will cheer

in the golden age when the poor
inherit the earth one apartment at a time
the multitudes have arrived a new world is rising
farms become tenements
immigrants become americans
who will rest who will eat who will work

who will raise families and ride that great train
to a modest job and home to a modest kitchen
commuters flicker past trackside windows
curtains flutter and the glass shakes
garlic and cabbage and old country recipes
simmer on the flames of freedom

green stanchions green stations
lady liberty has turned green above the gray water
the sidewalks are gray the tenements are brown
or white or gray or red and the street gets little sunlight
children play and laugh in the shadows
the el sparks and thunders and storms across the sky

III. 1955

the sons and daughters of immigrants
survived poverty and prohibition
the depression and two world wars
now their children are given dog tags
and schools teach to duck and cover
when atomic bombs explode

but the economy is booming
the city thrives and factories flourish
televisions toys cars
disneyland gunsmoke the mickey mouse club
mcdonald's opens in illinois and eisenhower
sends aid and advisors to vietnam

this humble train this noble artery of democracy
the bronx harlem yorkville
lenox hill murray hill
little italy and chinatown
in this land where liberty proudly enlightens the world
rosa parks is arrested and the boycott begins

the third avenue el is mortal it lives it moves
it dies a long slow death
the aquarium has been closed and the fish deported
ellis island is abandoned to rot in the harbor
on the final manhattan run people doff their hats
and toast the last echoes of its passing glory

IV. 1973

the once great el is merely
a minor shuttle an appendix
lost in the intestines of the bronx
the dodgers and giants have migrated west
the yankees wane and rust
mottles the rivets of industry

america the beautiful wrestles with itself
broken glass lost dreams
riots and assassinations
planned obsolescence and withdrawal with honor
the weary el clatters like a faithful milk wagon
while tenements crumble and die

the world trade center rises above the skyline
the last passenger run is made in the dark
and the train disappears in the night
the streets will be quiet and sidewalks
freed from shadow but the world
will not seem so wonderful

towers will rise where towers have fallen
the bronx will rise from the ruin
ellis island will reopen and the children
of the children of immigrants will come
to behold that great green lady
her colossal foot trampling forever the broken chain of slavery

her torch pointing to heaven
where stars are innumerable stations

and the great train rumbles toward paradise

standing upon the fordham road bridge

on a walk from nothing to do to nowhere to go
i stop here beneath heaven and above the harlem
river which curves from spuyten duyvil to hell gate
past the train yard and bus barn and power plant
through bluffs of tenement and project
in a valley veiled in concrete and night

all those little people with their big lives
all those big people with their little lives
asleep now or wandering the streets
searching for a cool breeze in the humid gloom
or cheap or expensive thrills which bring
forgetfulness of whatever pain there is to life

and i have found the river
darker and deeper it seems than space itself
though the sky is a gray haze of city light
which obscures the stars as we are obscured
and i stand above unheard currents
where tall masted ships no longer sail

i watch striations of light on the midnight water
which casts no human reflection
and tells no tales of what it carries away
the silent inscrutable current is a thirst
to be salted by unfathomable oceans
and in the depth of this drowning darkness

the faint vision of dawn
bringing a new day to this weary world

halloween

detroit burns and the bronx is mugged
with socks full of stones the wicked beat
money from mortal flesh
pirates and devils
torment candy from the naive

riots and thievery and war always war
there are no loving arms
strong enough to fend off the world
blood and grief and bloated bodies
children starve and the innocent die but tonight

the slaughtered will rise from sprawling graves
tonight urchins will drift across mine fields
their ghostly songs whine like artillery
and in mockery eggs splatter
like bombs from unseen rooftops

o do wear a mask of a monster or mutant
it is less hideous than to look
helpless into the face of humanity
there were saints and gods among us
and we killed them

blessed are the dead who have been purged
of cruelty and greed
they know what we have lost
forlorn paradise heaven uncreated
they know and they will come

the intentionally killed the merely neglected
they who should fear but who love nevertheless
they will come who have been liberated
from the perpetual procreation of pain and stolen joy
they will come and they will dance

look look their bliss wafts through the tangible
we smile and we pray that the children will be safe
let us feed the darling monsters coin and corn
we who are so generous and who will send yet more
souls suffering to their graves for our great blessing

ne cede malis: **poem for the seal of the borough of the bronx**

yield not to evil
meet misfortune boldly
wings spread
head cocked
beak in profile
one stern
alert eye
stares forth
the bald eagle is perched
atop the hemisphere
the stylized cupule
of an acorn
a triangular shield
where the sky is broken
by the straight beams
of a circular sun
whose indifferent eyes
surface over calm water
peace and liberty shining
on the ripples of commerce
and at the base
a small triangle
dark
almost insignificant
it is the land
of new hope and old tradition
behold it is the bronx
here unseen millions create their lives
and await their fate
in the scroll
the ominous motto
ne cede malis
yield not to evil
all is surrounded

by a festooned circle
a suggestion of universal harmony
the sun has eyebrows
it is all so placid
the sky is cloudless
the waters still
the land a mere shoreline
a speck in eternity
and the eagle
watches his back
a wary carnivore
in a troublesome world

washington comes to visit

he arrives at grandma's house
just off cypress avenue
but nana does not serve him a bowl of her soup
and poppop does not offer him a hand-rolled cigar
and dad does not take his picture
because they are not home
it is 1781 and even their home is not there
but the british are
and washington is scouting enemy positions
so the redcoats welcome him
with cannon fire
from harlem and randall's island and nearby ships
but the general
continues his visit and goes
to the shoe shine parlor on brook avenue
uncle al does not give him a free shine
mom and aunt jean are not standing in the doorway
aunt helen is not watching from her window
and grandfather does not run out
into 138th street as he does
to welcome roosevelt's motorcade
he shines the cops' shoes
so they let him shake
the hand of the beloved f.d.r.
but washington is not yet president
and the shoe shine parlor and 138th street
and cypress avenue and brook avenue are not there
though the millbrook is and so is the mill
and muskets fire and cannons roar
it is noisy as the fourth of july
and washington plans to attack manhattan
and bring peace and quiet to the neighborhood
but he marches to yorktown instead
and the rest is history

grandfather: a photograph

standing outside
the shoe shine parlor
a short man
in a long apron
brushes in hand
elbows bent
a gray face
an impatient smile
as if to say
hurry
take the picture
there is work to do
my customers are waiting

bootblacks on the loose

we are bootblacks on the loose
and we might be found
in jersey or north of the county line
on summer tuesdays we swim
at palisades amusement park
the world's largest salt water pool
we cling to the board beneath the waterfall
and lose ourselves in the briny roar
saturday night it's pepper steak
at a chinese restaurant in yonkers
or a burger at ho jo's
where uncle al tries to convince
the waitress that i am an unusually short thirty-one year old
looking for a date
thought i am thirteen and still wrestling with puberty
sunday afternoon it might be
the bowling alley by yankee stadium
or the billiard parlor on brook avenue
cousin billy is gifted with great strength
and an abundance of enthusiasm
he subdues the pins with brute force
he breaks the rack with a thunderbolt
scaring the balls into pockets
and he pounds the leather into a shine
while sandy finesses his strikes and sweet talks
the bank shots and coaxes the shoes
to perfection
i suck at everything but have fun anyway
i am learning to sweat my way through a shine
not the strongest
not the suavest
but i get the job done
i cannot outswim
uncle al though billy

can beat him at bowling
and sandy can beat him at pool
but al's arms are like tree trunks
he has been a bootblack
longer than the three of us have been alive
and no pair of shoes
can make him sweat
he loves to take us places
when we are not working
and to play gin rummy when it rains
and to lie in the sun
on the boardwalk at palisades
and smoke a cigar after lunch
while we wait
so we won't get cramps
the proper amount of time
between eating and swimming
is exactly how long it takes
for al to finish his cigar
so we watch the manhattan skyline
and boats on the hudson river
and women in bikinis
and we wish
the day would never end

al

his father was a bootblack
and he is a bootblack
shining shoes with graceful movements
a faint smile beneath his moustache
while big band music plays on the ancient radio

and when the brushes dance
over the leather he leans
slightly like a man
gently holding the waist of a woman
in a prohibition era ballroom

p.s. 43

jonas bronck elementary school
he settled in paradise
on the east bank of the harlem river
divinely guided to a virgin forest
of unlimited opportunity
that needed only an industrious hand
to make it the most beautiful
region in the world he claimed
but we grew up on streets without trees
and we gathered in the auditorium to watch
space flights on a black and white television
the stage had a mural
of the purchase of the bronx
guys in tight black suits and long white stockings
and some sachem outside a longhouse
the suits were not spandex
and the longhouse was not made
of barclay-barclite fiberglass panels
and just beyond the panorama
maybe some old lenape was saying
there goes the neighborhood
they are letting the whites in
they do not even speak the language
is that real money or are these guys just
a couple of broke tulip farmers with counterfeit wampum
when a launch was delayed we watched reruns
of *my little margie*
then it was back to the space race
because america must beat russia to the moon
so the commies would not invade the bronx
and we stockpiled tanks and troops in europe
and we saved the world for democracy
though we could not save the neighborhood
from drugs and crime

and in our kindergarten classroom
midnight vandals threw the teacher's coffee into the aquarium
the goldfish was floating belly up in the morning
no one talked us through our sadness and fear
it was a tough school
if you barfed in the cafeteria you had to clean it up yourself
which led to more barfing
you cleaned and barfed till you barfed no more
and there was nothing more to clean
then you went to class or went home
my mother had her own memories
of this educational institution
where teachers put clothes hangers
inside kids' shirts to encourage good posture
and criticized mom because her parents spoke italian
and not good english
so when they sent letters home in spanish
which neither she nor i could read
she shared her disgruntlement at the main office
but the next letter came again in spanish
and she returned again and again
she was quite good at expressing disgruntlement
in perfect bronx english
most of us were not bilingual but we were quick learners
in kindergarten we were not taught the alphabet
but the first grade teacher assumed we knew it
we learned this is the way life would always be
full of irony and incongruity and strange paintings
and of love and disgruntlement and rebellion
in third grade i became enamored
with a leopard skin coat
there was a redhead inside it
i don't remember her name
but what a coat

when they painted the doors pink
and put a DO NOT TOUCH sign on the wall
how could i resist
shoving my hat into the wet paint
they would not arrest me for it
they would not send me to the principal
the redhead would not be impressed
even my mother would not yell
at something so absurd
it was like the rich taking money from the poor
it was like going to the moon while the world was dying
it was like sending troops to vietnam
it was like arsonists burning tenements
even when the slumlords did not pay them
it was like writing poetry
instead of working on wall street
it was like jonas settling the bronx
and thinking he could improve paradise
it was because there was a sign
saying not to
it was because the tenements
were crumbling and the trees had vanished
and john wayne had killed all the indians
except for a few token sidekicks
it was because
it was there
and i had a hat
and the paint was wet
and i was a stupid kid
with a pink hat
receiving a great education
in america

cypress avenue

the avenue is named for the trees
that once grew in the morris arboretum
before the age of development and ruin
they are gone but their spirits linger
on this quiet avenue in the noisy bronx
a half mile of peace and simple wonder
or is it just childhood illusion
the thrill of saint mary's park
the lure of the randall's island walkway
the corner candy store
that sells joyva halvah and joyva joys
chocolate covered raspberry jelly bars
so tart and sweet even hamlet
would find succulence in the dull world
at grandmother's apartment her cooking
brightens the railroad flat
the aroma seeps out the window
and the street seems to sparkle
there is a green beauty salon
a turquoise shoe shine parlor
p.s. 65 with its light brown bricks
sparrows chirp in the schoolyard
and when the basketball courts are deserted
in the solitude of a sunday afternoon
even a clumsy kid
can pretend to be an all-star
the millbrook housing projects
are young and pink
christmas lights blink in various windows
i watch the flashing colors
to the point of insanity
while daddy warms up his 54 plymouth
in an outdoor parking lot by a scraggly locust tree sapling
as the car radio plays

wonderland by night
and i wonder
about the abandoned public school
p.s. 29 is bone white in the harsh sun
a spectral glow in the dark
the children say it is haunted
and i am a child
and in a long narrow store
lost in the red and yellow flames
of arson perhaps
father buys me the black knight of nurnberg
it is the missing piece
of my collection of aurora plastic models
the red knight of vienna
the blue knight of milan
the silver knight of augsberg
there is a gold knight of nice
i do not know it exists but it would be nice to have
i would lust for it as i did for the black knight
but my temporal desires have been temporarily satisfied
i am happy for a while
and safe for a while
in bed at night surrounded
by stuffed animals that protect me from bad dreams
while the knights keep watch from my shelves
there are tears and joy
there are more things to fear in heaven and earth
than i can dream of
as i glue together the armor
that protects me from the world

skully

we squat we crawl we kneel
we lie on the sidewalk to shoot
bottle caps from square to square
in a game that demands
intimate contact with the street
and we play it with a summer frenzy
on a worn slab of cement outside 514
smooth almost as hallway marble
the only one like it on the block
in the neighborhood in the known world
unmarred by cracks and even
the residue of long discarded chewing gum
has become one with the surface
a man-made stone made perfect by time
and we study the board with the intensity
of pool hall hustlers and we flick
the middle finger off the thumb
make the shot and go again
hit an opponent and advance
we grow calluses on fingers and palms
we wear holes in dungarees years before
it becomes fashionable
our knees blacken but we do not care about arthritis
and we do not care how stiff the iron-on patches feel
before we wear holes in them too
our mothers mend and sew
our fathers say
who do you think i am rockefeller
when we ask for a dime to buy soda
so we do not ask for new pants
they were children of the great depression
they are hard working men and if there is change
in their pockets we will get that orange nehi
and we will save the cap and fill it

with melted crayons and we will line up
and shoot away the summer afternoon
angling from square to square
one to four on each corner
five through twelve midway on each side
thirteen in the center
again and again we crisscross deadman's zone
and must avoid disaster
like our fathers went from poverty to war to the thankless jobs
they are grateful to have
like the big boys flirt
with drugs police crime paternity
they hope to get out of adolescence alive
and survive their unknown futures
there is a wall around berlin
the russians are building missile bases in cuba
and vietnam looms beyond the sunset of many childhoods
the line between victory and defeat is chalk thin
we must make that crucial shot
into the thirteenth box
dead center in deadman's zone
and live to tell about it

the tire man

nixon is rising and the yankees are falling
and i am walking to my political science class
i walk up the hill and down the hill
and a long way along fordham road
in my adolescent oblivion
and i stop
when a tire rolls across the sidewalk
i do not drive but i am a good pedestrian
i yield to rolling tires
even those not attached to cars
another tire follows it
and another
i see a tire lying on the ground
and the man in the back of a truck
drops a tire straight down so it hits
in just the right spot and rolls
across the sidewalk and up the ramp
to be caught and loaded onto the dock
they do not teach this in college so i watch
i cannot explain the vectors involved nor the probability
of repeatedly dropping a tire onto the exact spot
to give it sufficient momentum and an accurate path
i left the engineering program to become an english major
so the poetic beauty of it is enough for me
there are a few sliders and curves but the tires
always get to where they are going
and when the show is over i go to class
where tests are being returned and the professor says
i gave you 35 points for putting your name on the paper
because it is good to know your name
so how can one of you get a 42
i do not know who got the bad score
and i do not know the name
of the tire man

just another nondescript earning an honest living
he will never run for president
he will never pitch for the yankees
but there are no spitballs
and he throws a perfect game

a small but perfect world

at thanksgiving we give thanks
for all we take for granted
the turkey the lasagne
the ceiling over our head
our apartment in the south bronx
the bedrooms are small
the dining room is not
we gather and feast
and the table is cleared
soon construction begins
the plywood is covered in a green grass mat
tracks are laid out and screwed down and wired up
engines and cars are placed on the rails for a test run
then the landscape is made complete
a city hall a bank a hospital
suburban townhouses
a farmhouse a barn and pens for the livestock
cows and pigs and chickens and trees
little people sitting on benches
at the station or on lounge chairs
at the little motel or in a suburban backyard
or walking to the diner or to the mailbox
or waving lanterns beside switch towers
there are platforms for the unloading
of milk cans and logs
a radar tower and a light tower
a water tank and crossing signals
these are the toys my parents never had
during the depression
now dad works in the financial district
where the buildings are tall and the streets are narrow
crowded by day and deserted by night
and before the world trade center
there are clearing houses and discount shops

so the bargains come home
the landscape is filled in
and expanded to the tall buffet
connected to the lowlands by mountains
which mom makes by painting grocery bags
and crumpling them and shaping them
a beautiful illusion in the heart of reality
a small but perfect world
where the streets are clean
and nobody gets mugged on the way to the store
where no one sets buildings on fire
or dies of an overdose in a back alley doorway
it is like living in the land of *leave it to beaver*
a small but perfect world
where there is much to be thankful for
christmas comes and the new year is celebrated
then each illusion is put back into its box
and the dining room table
is again just the dining room table
and school reopens
the cold of january sets in
and we are
still
thankful

the fountain of youth

the sewer backed up and the street filled with glowing green water which all began when a neighborhood juvenile delinquent who was not very neighborly and who robbed from friend and foe alike like he just did not care lifted the manhole cover to show us the sights so we gathered to watch in awe brown walls of waterbugs writhing like times square on new year's eve and a few leapt up into daylight and into our nightmares for these were the winged tanks of the cockroach army whose armor mere sneakers could not destroy and we jumped back squealing and laughing then but not later and this neighborhood juvenile delinquent who was not very neighborly and who robbed from friend and foe alike like he just did not care liked to impress us so he threw seven milk crates perfectly suitable for sitting down the shaft but no one would sit in the street that hot summer night to talk and to watch the kids play punchball in the dark and there would be no open air games of dominoes or poker because the sewer backed up so much that the city sent a crew to repair it while we stood in the doorways to watch the strange sight of something actually getting fixed but things get worse before they get better the old timers always say and the maintenance crew flooded the sewer with dye which went down and came up and the waterbugs went down and the milk crates came up and the street filled with glowing green water which the maintenance men left like they just did not care so for a week no one played outside and the neighborhood juvenile delinquent hung out somewhere else and the shoppers and the commuters walked next to the buildings to avoid the chartreuse stench which took so long to recede that it became the evergreen symbol of what the city thought of us like it just did not care and of how we could not play on our own street which we would never forget though someday we might get lucky and hit the number or write a hit tune and move someplace where glowing green water would never happen somewhere like fifth avenue or sutton place where our bodies grow old and fat while our spirits drink immortal rage and compassion from the fluorescent green ooze of the waterbug writhing fountain of youth

III

… on the banks of brook avenue
where childhood is idyllic
and the world could not be more beautiful

welcome to the mainland

stagger from the atlantic's swell
seek land legs on ellis island
floundering through bureaucracy
and ferried to narrow streets awash
with humanity on the golden shores
of lower manhattan

the brooklyn bridge is a masterpiece
a magnificent temptation
but that alluring long island
stretches east and disintegrates
it points back to the world
you sailed so long to leave

now you migrate north
your ship has come and it has left
you tired and poor
yearning masses huddled and tossed
by the rattle and rock of the train
metal wheel upon metal rail

grinding and sparking
through the wonders of the city
beyond hell gate to paradise
where the tenements are young
where freedom is a peninsula
with heat and indoor plumbing

the brakes squeal the doors
to the new world open
welcome to the mainland welcome
to the bronx where all seems possible
here subways whoosh
underground and roar through the sky

there are rooms for rent
there is always room for one more
friend relative countryman
for one more lost soul
for one more exile
and the horizon fills with brick and glass

behind every silver window lies a dream
which may or may not be fulfilled
and in the cold snuggling of dark winter
or the wriggling of humid summer nights
babies are conceived and they are born
in america

this is not the land of your birth
though the native tongue remains
and the food tastes familiar
at dinner time that old world aroma
wafts through the hallway
the clatter of pots and pans

reverberates in the air shaft
where clotheslines sag with laundry
readied for the great
assimilation of work and school
backyard and alley echo
with multilingual profanity

prayers rise to the heavens
there are churches and synagogues
street corner preachers
rooms where idealists
contemplate utopia and the right
to believe or not to believe

there are times of prosperity
times of common despair
and always the children play
on sandlot and side street
in park and playground
they sing and cry and taunt and cheer

there are saloons and speakeasies
and saloons once again
ice cream parlors and candy stores
vaudeville and movies
all manner of entertainment
under the sun and under the moon

war will come and peace will come
again and again and there will be
parades and memorials and protests
you will grow old and remember
those days of struggle and joy
those friends relatives neighbors

lost in a changing world
where streets disappear and housing projects
spring forth like towers of babel
belgian blocks and trolley tracks
drown in rivers of asphalt
and moses parts the land

his great road cleaves its heart
there is exodus
poverty turmoil and tragedy
tenements burn and fall
there is rubble and more rubble
anger and desperation

ash and dust and broken bricks
and a spirit that suffers but does not die
and a hope that emerges
like weeds from the ruin
the survivors will fight
and new americans will come

the void will fill
with townhouses and pocket parks
there will be new music
new art and new words
and the aroma of exotic foods
will waft through the streets

fragrant and pungent
hopeful

and free

america's favorite pastime

and so it came to pass that the shortest kid in ninth grade was tired of the tallest kid in ninth grade not tired of the vertical difference but just tired of being pushed around so one bright sunny bronx morning the short kid came with a baseball bat and chased the tall kid around the schoolyard until the teachers took the bat and sent us all to class in this melting pot school where we did not quite fit the recipe so the bureaucracy batted us around and threw us curveballs like having us retake the reading test because our scores were too high and declaring 85 the passing grade and decimating our academically advanced class of those with hispanic surnames or dark skin but maybe this was still better than last year in that other school where gangs beat up anyone who was not violent like that quiet little spanish girl who ran crying and screaming down the hallway after the principal came into the classroom and announced the names of kids who were being kicked out of the program and being sent back to eighth grade in their respective ghetto schools but what did the principal care she was just a little girl from some other neighborhood and this is america this is social darwinism this is junior high school where only the strong survive like that short kid with the baseball bat that they took away but they could not stop him and after school he took out a baseball from his pocket and chased the tall kid all the way to the train station and is it not america's favorite pastime to watch big guys beating on little guys and little guys beating on big guys while spectators laugh and cheer glad they are not getting beat up and just hoping to survive

yankee fan

my cap is navy blue and boldly embroidered
with white interlocking letters
i bought it in my old neighborhood in the bronx
five bucks at a store on creston avenue
a converted newsstand that sells
handbags trinkets statues umbrellas
everything but candy and newspapers
yes the kids and i have inherited
my mother's love for a good bargain
and her loyalty to the home team
but the yankees are always on the road when we visit
so we cruise dollar stores and discount joints
and watch the game on television
and watch grandma watching the game
rooting for hits and home runs
putting whammies on opposing pitchers
screaming with the intensity
of a green bay packers fan when the bears are losing
and i wear my new york yankees baseball cap
all over madison wisconsin
where everyone is so politically correct
and motivated by humanitarianism or legislation
taught from childhood not to hurt anyone's feelings
and these friendly and sensitive midwesterners
are compelled to say hello to passersby
even those wearing new york yankee caps
but like some landlocked progeny
of the ancient mariner they must catch my eye
and tell me with compulsive conviction
that they hate the yankees
and i must smile and listen
to these hardworking middle americans
as they denounce good old american capitalism
at least as it applies to winning teams

but i am too polite to tell them
i mostly wear the cap to keep the sun out of my eyes
though i do have some recall
of kubek boyer and richardson
and an aging mantle hitting a home run
three balls two strikes two outs
in the bottom of the ninth *holy cow*
and mel stottlemyre's inside-the-park grand slam
but i was too young to understand the game
and when i was old enough to appreciate baseball
the yanks were so bad they had rocky colavito pitch
and the best catch i saw at the stadium
was made by a fat i mean overweight
i mean corporally-gifted woman
she had a straw hat three feet in diameter
and when the foul ball bounced off a box seat rail
she held up her hat and it went right in
she might have been from the midwest
or the grand concourse and who knows
where she bought that oversized beach hat
and that magnificent muumuu
the fans applauded the beauty of it
finally something to cheer about
and the right field grandstand
gave her a standing ovation
we wanted to offer her a contract
she was built like the bambino
and we needed a new superstar
instead we got a decade of despair
but how can i explain this to those who are compelled
to tell me that they hate the yankees
while i am compelled to listen
i who was raised in the era
before lawyers and psychologists and sensitivity training

raised in an environment so insensitive
it invented the bronx cheer
i who do not hate the cubs or the brewers
though i will not watch the braves
after all those america's team commercials
because this is america and no american
should be told who to root for
and that smiley faced cleveland indians' logo
is too offensive even for my politically incorrect taste
but i do not explain this
it would take too long and these friendly
fellow americans might ask
about my brooklyn accent
even though i am from the bronx
just like the yankees so i let them talk
and when their strange power of speech
is done and they are once again
congenial madisonians
i simply reply
the more you hate us the more we love it
the more you boo us the more fun it is to win

the gambling leaguers

cheer of crowd crack of bat slap of leather
what beauty in the grace of the great
in the arc of arm of ball of leaping body
the skillful passion of these sandlot ballers
these gambling leaguers these seasonal warriors
waging serious sport in parks and playgrounds
on diamonds of clay or asphalt
against a background of bridge and school
of factory and tenement
a colorful panorama of the ordinary
no one asks for autographs
just victory over the tedium of work and bills
and the urban summer's ceaseless heat
this childhood game fought with adult intensity
for stakes of fifty or a hundred per position or more
side bets among spectators and the excitement begins
the fans live and die in suspense
the winners are rich the losers poor
celebration and frustration and the promise
of the next game the next season
so they play till the money runs out
till legs no longer run till arms no longer throw
with the speed and strength of youth and they fade
into the bleachers to wait
to play again perhaps
where summer is eternal
and the umpires
omniscient

lost again on old subways

i am lost again on old subways
at third avenue station the lights go out
the lunatic laughs
the lunatic who does not appear
until the lights go out
and i cannot see him
and i cannot see what he is laughing at
he laughs and he laughs
death is solemn
but suffering is hysterical
when it happens to others
the three fates the three stooges
torturing each other while the children laugh
until the lights go out and they are stuck
in their own nightmares
and he laughs at my fear
and i laugh at him laughing at my fear
because i am afraid not to
keep the lunatic happy
i have paid my fare and i must journey
there is nowhere to go but where the darkness takes me
and i must get my money's worth
the doors will not open
i cannot depart at the home station
and i slip past my sleeping parents
under the bronx and over the bronx
all the unseen passengers on this runaway train
are laughing and laughing
because we are afraid to stop
we are lost in the bronx
where guns will not save us
and the churches are closed for the night
and the candles lit for the souls of the dead
have burned out and the priests

have locked the rectories
and we are laughing too hard to pray
and we are laughing so hard we almost enjoy it
we have transformed we are the laughing commuters
of the IRT which never looked so good
though we cannot see it as it trembles on
through the night which does not stop
through strange territories where strangers lurk
in the shadows waiting for a few laughs

randall's island

I

here the sky is blue and the water dark
and the bronx an invisible memory
here clouds roll off the continent
goodbye goodbye go rain upon the old world
should it still exist

here the new city greets ancient tides
at the corner of harlem and hell gate
and distinctions obscure
where is the end where is the beginning
how many have drowned like names in the wind

chaotic currents chaotic streets
the orderly megalithic shoreline
of a fishdead metropolis
a horizontal stonehenge on which to celebrate
existence and the rats seem to dance

i cast my bait into the emptiness
launch my kite to the sun
no fish to catch no one to meet
this is a forgotten island
obscure as childhood

II

the confluence of memory and dream
this prehistoric erosion from the mainland
a muddle of time and amazing eternity
there are moments when dandelions roar
in sunlight like british muskets

when summer grass shimmers
as if the present were luminous
while churning and dark the currents
muffle all sound and the unheard
skyline rises to the unspeaking heavens

the delinquent cursed at toil and at play
the institutionalized soul
screamed with rage and frustration
in the infants' hospital the foundling cried
and succumbed to quiet death

the house of refuge the idiot asylum the orphanage
razed and forgotten
and the triborough bridge rises
above park and playground and stadium
amid the wayward whispers of these outcast lands

III

green ticket booths and silver railings
the bleachers are empty and in the plaza
the bronze discus thrower stands naked and alone
trimmed hedges low walls red brick
i balance between fantasy and failure

beneath the pillars of the viaduct
i learn my clumsy insignificance
this is a sacred place and we bury
songless parakeets in shoe boxes after they die
and launch plastic rockets to the virgin moon

between fact and delusion the line has vanished
the little hell gate has drowned in the garbage landfill
the bridge to the psychiatric hospital
stands irrelevant over a river of grass
and rabbits run mad across evening fields

what insane dreams wander the wasteland
darkness drizzles and night
awakens the restless tenements
wisps of arson smog the horizon and i must return
i must and it seems

even i am not here

triborough bridge: suspension

    the

    sky

    road rises

    quickly above green

    shores and gray waters

from astoria to wards island from anchorage to massive anchorage

    graceful cables curve

    sturdy

    blue

    arches

    crowned

    with art deco lanterns

atop steel towers that aspire to heaven above the turbulent hell gate

    bearing the stress of humanity

    festooning the night

    with man

    made

    stars

triborough bridge: stasis

where is everybody going
the best part of this bridge is the middle
between here and there
between above and below
between all the points
on the invisible compass
of our existence
between scylla and charybdis
to the east the solemn frown
of the railroad bridge over the bucolic hell gate
to the west the land of opportunity and misfortune
the magnificent skyline
a forest of penthouse and project
where the homeless home in the shadows
humanity is beautiful from a distance
the landfills bloom with green growth
frivolous waves drown the effluence
of the money mad world
to the north the sewage treatment plant
that will never make us clean
and the manhattan psychiatric hospital
and the center for the criminally insane
and the abandoned asylum
where inmates laughed at pedestrians
as they walked across the sky
in the longago days of carefree strolls
before random violence
before muggings in broad daylight
the happy people of wards island
picnic beneath trees
to the south children splash
in the clear blue water of astoria pool
imagining that they are sharks
or whales or submarines

imagining that summer will never end
reality is such an imposition
like the grim stone of the war memorial
just beyond their youthful laughter
and above restless clouds drive by
on their ceaseless commute
below there is bedlam and mayhem and the tides
swirl over suicides and shipwrecks
but here in the middle there is peace
there is stasis
there is the music
of wind murmuring through cables
why must every polluted river be crossed
here words are invisible
and the past is no more
the future is but the loss of the present
leap to the sky
not to fly
jump to the water
never to swim again
walk ashore
to live and die in the eternal city
where the meek await to inherit
what is left of the earth
o the hovering the hovering

triborough bridge: genesis

in the beginning there was the land and the water
the water separated the mainland from the islands
and moses said *may there be a great bridge*
to join the islands to the islands and the islands to the mainland
it was good and moses said
may there be roads and highways that lead to the great bridge
that joins the islands to the islands and the islands to the mainland
it was good and moses said
may there be parks and playgrounds
for the people in the cars that drive
on the roads and highways that lead to the great bridge
that joins the islands to the islands and the islands to mainland
it was good and moses said
may there be money to build the great bridge
and the roads and highways and parks and playgrounds
and behold there was money
the nation went to work and it was good
the steel industry lit its furnaces and factories reopened
loggers logged and sawmills sawed
railroads hauled lumber across the continent
laborers constructed wooden forms and poured cement
barges ferried girders over the water and towers rose
cables were wound and anchored
the deck suspended and the roadway paved
the great bridge joined the islands to the islands
and the islands to the mainland
there were parks and parkways and the president
came for the opening ceremony
and the people came and rushed to be first
to pay the toll and cross the great bridge
and more people came to pay the toll
more people and more money
money that could be used to build more bridges
and it was all good
but moses did not rest

triborough bridge: kinesis

an automobile vortex
where three bridges meet
twelve directions of traffic
twenty-two lanes that do not intersect
cars can go from here to there to another there
this is america and there are tolls
to pay and toll booths to collect the money
and police to collect those who do not pay the toll
but we kids are oblivious to the wonders of engineering
and we have no money to give to trolls
we run and scream and fight monsters
in the cement towers of the bronx span
we want to ascend the spooky staircase
and explore the walkway to manhattan
but mommy herds us to the playground on randall's island
where she can sit in the shade and talk to the matron
while the cars whirl overhead
and harry sits on his hill
a small patch of grass bordered by an access ramp
beneath the grand junction
where the harlem span meets the viaduct
harry in his undershirt
drinking his quart of beer hidden in a brown paper bag
basking in the sun and alone in the quiet
he does not build bridges
he does not have a car
he works hard and dies in poverty
they give his ashes to the winds
and he intersects
with everywhere in the great universe
as cars speed by
and the commuters take no notice

astoria park

the memorial is a tombstone
gray as war
gray as the hell gate's insane tides
gray as the triborough's symmetry
gray as the psychiatric hospital's lobotomized windows
gray as the railroad's commerce
gray as the skyline of the glorious city
gray as the storm we watched
father and son from the concrete bleachers
the crowd ran from the pool
raindrops splashed on the chlorine
we sat in the gray rain
we sat together

the dead are not buried here
they are gone as are the dolphins
which led the dutchman up this strait
intoxication and shipwreck
visions of the devil dancing on his stones
new amsterdam is gone
the indians are gone
this east river is toxic
it flows north and south
it never was a river
daddy tells stories of sunken treasure ships
we will never be rich
we will never be but what we are

father and son
forever in the gray rain
with our pot bellies and our pale skin
and our tender feet and our anxieties
our lifetimes of work and responsibility
maybe the car window is open

maybe the apartment is burning down
maybe the boss does not like us
and we will be sucked into homeless poverty
like locker keys into hungry drains beneath waveless waters
our possessions lost in bureaucracy
in america where the rivers are poison
and there are no free swims

this pool was built for the huddled masses
doff those work clothes and be free
bathing suit naked
beneath the lightning before the wind
in a distant memory of childhood
the iron bars keep us safe
we will not walk into the wine dark tides
of the hell gate and never return
we simply do not leave
at night underwater lights shine
like the new jerusalem
the gray sky darkens with stars
the spirit rises over radiant water

we simply will not leave

the banks of brook avenue

and brook avenue runs
straight through the crooked world
from railroad yard
north to the meat market
and curves and disappears
into the heart of the bronx
where tenements burn and die
and stare black eyed and hollow
like the dead waiting for the soul to rise
and america flies to the moon
and america drops bombs
and america makes war on crime and drugs
but brook avenue never ends
the old mill stream flows long buried
in the great sewer beneath the great street
of the great borough of the bronx
where founding fathers sleep
beneath the shadows of saint ann's church
and indian villages deconstruct
beneath abandoned factories
and the belgian paving stones on which horses clopped
lie beneath the asphalt where automobiles drift
from the bronx kill to the american mainland
and the millbrook housing projects rise to the heavens
above tarpaper roofs where pigeons and junkies
forget their way home
and the brook babbles beneath the surface
and the brook finds its way through the underworld
to the ocean that brings
immigrants to the new continent
they build skyscrapers and railroads
they fight wars and they play baseball
they make money and move to the grand concourse
they make more money and move to the suburbs

or they remain impoverished and searching
for brook avenue grass for brook avenue women
for a steady man for a steady job
for the ship that sails to paradise
the winters are cold in unheated apartments
fire hydrants flood the summer streets with toddlers
and on the banks of brook avenue i see
the world as it is
and the sun beats down
and the bootblacks toil and sweat drops from their brows
and the bootblacks beat beauty into old shoes
and the bootblacks earn a living one dollar at a time
in america where we vote for our kings
and the police beat whom they wish
and the strong beat the weak
and the women walk to store to church to playground
and the children play beneath shady tenements
where boughs of streetlights
do not dance in the wind
and the children laugh and the children cry
on the banks of brook avenue
and the sun sets and the night rises
and the pool hall grows smoky and serious
and the children dream and the children have nightmares
and the darkness of heaven and the darkness of civilization
and the sighs of the lonely and the sighs of lovers
are indistinguishable
on the banks of brook avenue
where childhood is idyllic
and the world could not be more beautiful

Bibliography: Previous Publications {from the banks of brook avenue}

avenue b, 14th street, looking south
You Are Here: New York City Streets in Poetry. P & Q Press. 2006.
Z Miscellaneous. Winter 1989.

the beach beneath the bridge
North Coast Review. Issue 7, 1995.

the fountain of youth
The Prose Poem: An International Journal. Vol. 2, 1993.

the gambling leaguers
The Glacier Stopped Here: an anthology of poems by Dane County writers. Dane County Cultural Affairs Commission & Isthmus Publishing. 1994.

grandfather: a photograph
The Spirit That Moves Us. Vol. 6, no. 1, 1981.

justice
Live Lines: Is There a Place for Poetry in Your World? Pearson Canada Inc. 2011.
And Justice For All. Perfection Learning Company. 2000.
Welcome to Your Life: Writings for the Heart of Young America. Milkweed Editions. 1998.
The Party Train: A Collection of North American Prose Poetry. New Rivers Press. 1996.

lost again on old subways
Tokens: Contemporary Poetry of the Subway. P & Q Press. 2003.

ne cede malis: poem for the seal of the borough of the bronx
The Bronx County Historical Society Journal. Vol. XLV, nos. 1 & 2, spring/fall 2008.

on the coping
Dusty Dog. Vol. 2, no. 1, January 1991.

standing upon the fordham road bridge
Connections: New York City Bridges in Poetry. P & Q Press. 2012.
North Coast Review. Issue 7, 1995.

triborough bridge: suspension
POETS on the line. No. 3, spring 1996.

yankee kitchen
This is an elaboration of a short poem, **genghis khan,** which appeared in *Wormwood Review.* Vol. 33, no. 3, 1993.

www.ingramcontent.com/pod-product-compliance
Lightning Source LLC
Chambersburg PA
CBHW030234240426
43663CB00036B/354